LIVING JESUS
OUT LOUD

Also by Lonnie Honeycutt:

Death, Heaven and Back:
The True Story Of One Man's Death
And Resurrection

LIVING JESUS OUT LOUD

True Life Stories for Real Life Ministry

by

Lonnie Honeycutt

WHP

Wyatt House Publishing
www.wyattpublishing.com

Wyatt House books may be ordered through booksellers or by contacting:

WYATT HOUSE PUBLISHING
399 Lakeview Dr. W.
Mobile, Alabama 36695
www.wyattpublishing.com

Because of the dynamic nature of the Internet, any web address or links contained in this book may have changed since publication and may no longer be valid. The views expressed in this book are solely those of the author and do not necessarily reflect those of the publisher, and the publisher hereby disclaims any responsibility for them.

Cover design by: Sydney Bataller
sydney.bataller@yahoo.com

Author photo courtesy of Bill Starling
starlingphoto@me.com
www.starlingphoto.net

ISBN 13 TP: 978-0-9882209-0-4
ISBN 13 Ebook: 978-0-9882209-1-1

Library of Congress Control Number: 2012950908

Printed in the Untied States of America

Dedicated to:

- Eddie Honeycutt, my mother, for going through the living nightmare of raising me and for introducing me to the love of Jesus by living Him out to my brothers and sisters and me.

- Dawn Honeycutt, my wife, for loving me through the darkest hours of my life and death and for being a living embodiment of unconditional love.

- Melvin Badon and Libby Badon (Dad and Mom) for being tremendous examples of what it means to be grace-filled and for 'adopting' my family into their own.

- My children, Brance and Danielle, who, by their very existence, make me want to be a better example of Jesus.

"After observing Brother Lonnie and 99 for 1 Ministries for several years, I have come to the conclusion that 99 for 1 Ministries is what Jesus' ministry may have looked like when He was on earth. No big church building, none of the typical trappings of a church – just a group of people full of the love of Jesus, searching out the lowest of the low, under bridges, in alleys and in what I consider dangerous places – sharing the love of Jesus with the invisible people. While it's uncomfortable for most of us to look at these usually dirty, smelly people (people most of us avert our eyes and walk away from when we see them) 99 for 1 Ministries actively searches them out and shows them the true love of Jesus."

-Bob Glass, Former Alabama State Senator,
member of Gospel Way Baptist Church

"I first met Lonnie at a business meeting in 1999. Literally, within seconds of meeting for the first time, we were joyfully talking and sharing our testimonies of our lives in Christ and did so for an hour before any business was discussed. Our friendship grew and I became very close with his family. Lonnie's severe cancer as well as his eventual death and heaven experience had a huge impact on me as I saw the true personal 'Hand of God' in all of our lives. However, the most impressive part for me is working with Lonnie in 99 for 1 Ministries. I watch Lonnie and his radical heart for God's glory, being worked out every day in 99 for 1 Ministries as we minister to the hurting, helpless and those who just need a hand – all while trying to allow them to see and experience the love and hope of Jesus Christ. Lonnie's life purpose and daily aid to others and the work of 99 for 1 Ministries is the best example of what we read in James 1:22-27 – 'Be doers of the Word, and not hearers only... pure religion and undefiled before God the Father is this, to visit the fatherless, the orphans, and widows in their affliction, *and* to keep himself unspotted from the world.'"

-David Easterbooks, National Sales and
Marketing Manager, Board member of 99
for 1 Ministries, member of St. Patrick
Catholic Church of Carlsbad

"When 99 for 1 Ministries is on our calendar, I know that my clients are in for a blessing. Pastor Lonnie takes every opportunity to share the love of Jesus with ladies that have made a commitment to recovery. Being treated like a lady is a new experience for most of these women. Pastor Lonnie arranges frequent hair and make-up days, followed by a photo session (called a Day of Beauty). For many women, these pictures are the evidence of a new life in Christ – they are quite a change from the mug shots that were the only pictures they possessed. The Christmas party at our Recovery program hosted by this group is a highlight of our season. From being an outcast from family and society to being the honored guest at a party, is a blessing to all of us. Pastor Lonnie truly understands what it means to be the hands and feet of Jesus to a hurting world."

-Jeanne Harred, Director of the Haven of Hope for Women, member of Woodridge Baptist Church

"Pastor Lonnie and I have never met face to face yet I've shared and cried with him more than I have with any other person before. He's become a big brother to me and we've become the best of friends. I met Lonnie after sending him a question about a video I'd seen on Youtube concerning how he'd died and came back to life. To my utter surprise, he actually contacted me. One of the things that most impressed me about him is that he didn't care that I'd been homeless or that I'd served several years in prison. His testimony has helped me become an anchor for my family and 99 for 1 Ministries has helped our family grow closer to God. If I were asked 'Who has inspired you the most to serve the Living God,' I would definitely say it has been Lonnie because he truly lives Jesus out loud. Having read an advanced copy of Living Jesus Out Loud I can wholeheartedly endorse what is taught within its pages."

-Shane St. John, President of S & W Coordination, member of Mountain Life Assemblies of God

"My husband, Melvin, and I have known Lonnie and Dawn for a bit over seven years. They and their children have become like our own family. After he was ordained, Lonnie planted a church, developed cancer and, eventually, died. We were there for this last event and while it could have been traumatic, God used what could have been evil for good. Lonnie returned to us with memory loss that continues today but he was led by the Holy Spirit to begin 99 for 1 Ministries and it has flourished. Lonnie and Dawn are true examples of people who try to Live Jesus Out Loud. They love others unconditionally and, better still, they help others learn how to do the same."

-Libby and Melvin Badon,
Elder, Deeper Life Fellowship

"If anyone can write about 'Living Jesus Out Loud' it's Pastor Lonnie Honeycutt. I met Pastor Lonnie two years ago through a ministry project he was doing at The Haven of Hope for Women, a recovery program for women struggling with drugs/alcohol addiction. Pastor Lonnie's ministry, 99 and 1 ministries, was treating our ladies to a day of makeovers which included haircuts, make-up and photo shoots. Pastor Lonnie's heart for helping people from all walks of life is inspirational and demonstrates Jesus' plan for all his followers."

-Julie Reed, Program Manager of the Haven of
Hope for Women, member of First Baptist
North Mobile

"99 for 1 Ministries is not just any ordinary ministry. The ministry does a number of different things for many people. But my favorite thing is the outreaches that we do at the Haven of Hope (a drug and alcohol recovery center for women) and Tent City (a campsite for the homeless). 99 for 1 Ministries is a pure example of the saying "Love God, Love

People" and I am so glad that the Lord has put me in the path of Pastor Lonnie – someone who has become a great friend to me and my family."

-James Buck, Civil Estimator, Board Member of 99 for 1 Ministries, member of Bay Community Church

"I've known Lonnie Honeycutt for a number of years and through everything, he has been resolute to do everything he could to help others in the name of Jesus Christ. He has been faithful to the work God has given him to do, he is a faithful father and husband. 99 for 1 Ministries is reaching out to others with the love of God and is making a difference. While others talk a lot about helping, 99 for 1 Ministries is doing it. Pastor Lonnie is energetic, fun to be around, always looking for someone to bless (especially the poor and down and out) and he always lives Jesus out loud."

-Carl Lapane, Electrical Engineer, member of Deeper Life Fellowship

"Lonnie is the best example of a person who takes Jesus's words seriously and puts them into action. 'I was hungry and you gave me food. I was thirsty and you gave me drink. I was a stranger and you welcomed me. I was naked and you clothed me. I was sick and you visited me. I was in prison and you came to me... When you did it to one of the least of these, my brothers, you did it unto Me.'"

-Janet Stephens, School Teacher and Pastor's Wife, Cobbtown Christian Church

"As a long distance supporter of 99 for 1 ministry, I have been challenged and encouraged as I read the newsletters and hear the many ways that people are encountering God through this ministry. Pastor Lonnie's example of loving people unconditionally has challenged me to open my eyes and heart to the people in my own community. I have learned to reach out to strangers and offer prayer, a ride or a simple meal in a bag in the name of Jesus. Knowing what the 99 for 1 ministry is doing in Mobile and other parts of Alabama has challenged me to be bold for Jesus here in Washington."

-Reba Sanborn, Sunday School Teacher,
Olympic Vineyard Christian Fellowship

"Pastor Lonnie and 99 for 1 Ministries has led by example what it means to love others the way Jesus intended us to. Whenever I read the ministries newsletters or Lonnie's testimonies, I get inspired by the humanity that is shown and want to improve myself with the same attitude. In addition, Lonnie has shown me Jesus' love by ministering to me. I first "bumped into" Lonnie on Youtube when I saw his Heaven testimony. I decided to email him questions about his Heaven testimony, not expecting a reply. To my pleasant surprise, he took the time and effort to write me an extensive reply to my questions. In addition, he called me the next day to answer more questions and addressed the challenges I was having in my life at the time – all around his busy schedule! I appreciated the attention, and it was all centered on Jesus and the Gospel."

-David Wu, Cantonese and English Interpreter,
member of Southport Community Church

"Pastor Lonnie is a living example of what it really means to follow Christ. He reaches out to the hurting, helpless and often rejected, meeting their physical and spiritual needs. He leads people to Jesus by simply loving them and being their friend. I have been touched by his ministry. Being around him and seeing how he ministers to people gives me a desire to do more to help others."

-Angie Greene,
*Lead Singer, **Remaining Nameless,***
member of Jubilee Baptist Church

"Reverend Lonnie Honeycutt and 99 for 1 Ministries perfectly epitomize and embody this book's title. I personally do not know of, nor have I ever heard of a person who so tirelessly and selflessly gives, works and serves – no, loves – like Lonnie Honeycutt, his family, and this ministry. I have often heard the expression, "Jesus in the flesh." That should be Lonnie's nickname."

-Gary Morris, Elder, Deeper Life Fellowship

"Volunteering with 99 for 1 Ministries has opened my eyes to the needs of this world more than my 15+ years experience working as a professional social worker. Pastor Lonnie's heart to serve the "under-loved" truly amazes me. He reaches out to those in need by showing the love that our Lord has for every one of us and validates that we are all worthy of His love. Many of those served by our ministry have never felt worthy of anything and have lived through circumstances that most of us cannot even imagine. After being touched by the love of God through 99 for 1 Ministries, many feel hope for the first time in their lives."

-Carolyn A. Wesson, Licensed Master Social Worker, member of Deeper Life Fellowship

"Pastor Lonnie and 99 for 1 Ministries is an inspiration to many – from the ladies of the Haven of Hope who have drug and alcohol addiction issues to people most of us would be afraid to talk to – they are all loved on as if they were regular members of a church or life-long friends. Thank God we have ministries like this to go out and preach the gospel and bring many to the Lord. So many of us are caught up with daily life it's difficult to make the kind of impact that I have personally witnessed with 99 for 1 Ministries. I am so proud to know Pastor Lonnie because he is so passionate and willing to help those in need and to show everyone that we can positively impact the lives of others if we'll simply be aware of God's calling."

-Dr. Teresa Roberson, CEO My Nutrition Source, member of North Fayette Baptist Church

"As a social worker for the aged, I have seen a dramatic increase in homelessness during the past several years. I had been praying to Jesus to show me a way to help. One day, while I was counseling the elderly at a local food pantry, Pastor Lonnie sat down, introduced himself and asked if I had a few minutes to talk to him about helping those who are homeless in our community. That was the beginning of my becoming part of 99 for 1 Ministries as a volunteer social worker. Pastor Lonnie has been a great mentor to me. He has shown me how to practice true, Christ-like kindness and love to those who are homeless, living in tents, in cars and on the streets. Better still, instead of simply being there for these people, we've been instrumental in finding permanent homes for many of those we minister to."

-Stacey Hensley, Social Worker for Baldwin County Council on Aging, member of Celebration Community Church

"It has been my distinct privilege to walk with Lonnie and his family for almost 10 years. It became evident to me quickly, and has become proven out many times over the years, that Lonnie is gifted to see the invisible, to love the unloved, and to not only be the hands and feet of Jesus to the hurting, but to train others to be the same."

*-Dr. Mark A. Wyatt, pastor, Deeper Life Fellowship, author of **The New Normal: Experiencing the Unstoppable Move of God**, and **Hog Washed: a small fable about a big change***

Table of Contents

15

INTRODUCTION

As I begin this book I'd like to say I'm extremely aware that, due to the nature of the stories I'll share within (i.e., testimonials about those I've met and been allowed to minister to as well as personal stories that involve my family), some may consider me to be an egomaniac. To this I can only say that I'm not and that those who know me would, hopefully, agree.

The fact of the matter is that 'living Jesus out loud' is something I've been trying to do for over two decades now. Obviously, I was inspired to live this type of life by someone else and it's my most sincere hope that through the stories I'll share others will be inspired to do the same.

Speaking of inspiration, I came up with this book's title because of three people – one historical and two contemporary personalities. The historical figure is Saint Francis of Assisi who said, "**Preach the Gospel at all times and when necessary use words**."

I've always considered this suggestion to be brilliant because it sums up, succinctly and memorably, James 2:14-26 which states: "*What good is it, my brothers and sisters, if someone claims to have faith but has no deeds? Can such faith save them? Suppose a brother or a sister is without clothes and daily food. If one of you says to them, "Go in peace; keep warm and well fed," but does nothing about their physical needs, what good is it? In the same way, faith by itself, if it is not accompanied by action, is dead. But someone will say, 'You have faith; I have deeds.' Show me your faith without deeds, and I will show you my faith by my deeds. You believe that there is one God. Good! Even the demons believe that— and shudder. You foolish person, do you want evidence that faith without deeds is useless? Was not our father Abraham considered righteous for what he did when he offered his son Isaac on the altar? You see that his faith and his actions were working together, and his faith was made complete by what he did. And the scripture was fulfilled that says, 'Abraham believed God, and it was credited to him as righteousness,' and he was called God's friend. You see that a person is considered righteous by what they do and not by faith alone. In the same way, was not even Rahab the prostitute considered righteous for what she did when she gave lodging to the spies and sent them off in a different direction? As the body without the spirit is dead, so faith without deeds is dead."*

In short, I believe that St. Francis was telling us to live the faith we have in Jesus out loud – not just in word but through our deeds. As such, I prefer to preach by serving.

The second person who inspired the title is a missionary Baptist preacher, Raymond Whitely. When I met Ray I thought for certain he was a stereotypical 'Bible thumper' (someone who uses the Bible to try and bash you into submission – which never truly works). I thought this because Ray didn't believe in drinking alcohol, smoking, sleeping around, chewing gum and about a dozen other things that I had very little problems with. Obviously I'm exaggerating a bit (as far as I know Ray had nothing against chewing gum) but I hope you get my point. Ray told me that he stood against things that the world found acceptable. But, then, he did something I'd never seen any other Christian do… he actually lived out his beliefs. In other words, since he didn't believe in smoking or drinking or carousing, Ray didn't do those things. I found that I respected him for living out his convictions even though, at the time, I didn't agree with them. So, when he challenged to ask God if He were real and, if so, to reveal Himself to me, I accepted the challenge. It was a challenge that ended with my having a completely changed life (now and in eternity).

The third person who influenced the title of this book is the late singer/songwriter David M. Bailey. I wish I'd had the chance to meet David before he died. Unfortunately I didn't. Fortunately, David left behind a legacy of spirit-filled songs – songs infused with the spirit of the truth of Scripture.

'*Swan Song,*' in particular, had a very potent impact on me. The stanza that truly spoke to me was: "*So we built this shrine to the ones who passed away. It won't bring 'em back no matter how we pray. Some of them were good, some of them were bad, some made us smile, others made us mad. I wonder if they knew before they passed along that what we'd remember most is their swan song?*"

David's voice is one that practically no one could call 'beautiful' but, the soul-full-ness of the songs he sings more than makes up for his lack of vocal range and the playfulness of some of his lyrics simply makes me smile. David is a brother-in-the-Lord and I look forward to the day I can hug and thank him in person for following the Lord's direction in singing to all of us.

As you read this book I'd like you to keep the following in mind: While the stories, anecdotes and recollections you'll find within were personally experienced by or shared with me, I (we) give ALL the glory that may come about from the same to our Lord, Savior and Redeemer – Jehovah!

Beware: If you are not a Christian who is sold-out to the Lord Jesus Christ and who doesn't mind shouting the same from the rooftops; someone who believes that the Word of God is true yesterday, today and tomorrow – in its entirety – and can be taken to mean what it says and to say what it means, you will probably not like this book.

But, as a friend of mine says, "*You should give it a go.*" You never know. The book you hold in your hands (or are reading on a screen) may be one you quickly forget or it may be one God uses to stimulate the way you think about His Kingdom.

It's my prayerful hope that *Living Jesus Out Loud* will help you learn 'Why You Should' bless people with the knowledge and understanding you have about God.

If even one of the illustrations of how Christ has impacted, touched and shaped the lives of those we've encountered gives you an idea that enables or inspires you to witness to someone, all the pages I've written will have been worth the effort.

Two Important Notes

In many of the personal testimonies you'll notice that I'm able to actually provide quotes from those with whom I was talking. The reason I'm able to be so accurate is because I often had a recording device (hand-held or on my laptop) that I used to take notes. In the cases where I have to paraphrase what was said I do my best to be as accurate as possible.

I've chosen to change the names of most of those I reference herein for two reasons:

1) Testimonies are highly personal and I want to respect everyone's privacy.

2) In some cases those I reference could possibly be put in harm's way should their family, friends or even certain authorities find out that they've converted to Christianity.

Chapter 1

Living Jesus Out Loud Will Positively Impact Your Family

When asked what living Jesus out loud means, I answered:

"Live out the two greatest commandments that Jesus said completed the Law and Prophets (paraphrased): Love the Lord your God with all your heart, with all your soul, with all your strength and with all your mind; and love your neighbor as yourself. Do this and you will truly live Jesus out loud."

Living Jesus Out Loud is less of a 'How To' book than a 'Why You Should' book. The reason is simple: When people reach for a 'How To' book they expect to get step-by-step instructions on how to do whatever it is they're wanting to learn to do. That this is the case, even with evangelism, can been seen by the number of books written about the subject in the past two decades: Evangelism Explosion, The Master Plan of Evangelism, The Way of the Master, Complete Evangelism Guidebook, etc.

Since God has seen fit to make each of us dynamic individuals, cookie-cutter formulas rarely ever work – at least not long-term. Thus, it would be downright silly to believe that there's a one-size fits all approach to evangelism.

The difference between the concepts found in *Living Jesus Out Loud* and most other evangelism books on the market is that I want you, the reader, to capitalize on the strongest asset God has given you to demonstrate His love to others – your life.

People inspect the lives of those who call themselves Christians and decide not only whether we are genuine Christians but if Jesus is worth their attention. If for no other reason, we must be willing to be introspective about our lives and determine whether or not we're truly demonstrating the love of Christ through the way we live.

Having spoken with hundreds of pastors and thousands of parents from around America, as well as being aware of the research that's been done concerning children from Christian households who drop-out of organized religion once they've entered adulthood, I share the same concerns about the continued faith of my kids as I'm certain you do for your own children.

However, knowing what I do about the reasons given by those who have left organized religion, I'm confident that displaying the love of Jesus with passion, conviction and consistency is vital to keeping the focus of our children on Jesus.

The reason: Living for Jesus inspires us to live out the love He has placed in our hearts for others. This is important is because, according to a Barna-based poll (*Six Reasons Young Christians Leave Church*, 9-28-11), the top two reasons young people walk away from the corporate church are:

#1 – Churches seem overprotective. A few of the defining characteristics of today's teens and young adults are their unprecedented access to ideas and worldviews as well as their prodigious consumption of popular culture. As Christians, they express the desire for their faith in Christ to connect to the world they live in. However, much of their experience of Christianity feels stifling, fear-based and risk-averse. One-quarter of 18- to 29-year-olds said "Christians demonize everything outside of the church" (23% indicated this "completely" or "mostly" describes their experience). Other perceptions in this category include "church ignoring the problems of the real world" (22%) and "my church is too concerned that movies, music, and video games are harmful" (18%).

#2 – Teens' and twenty-somethings' experience of Christianity is shallow.

A second reason that young people depart church as young adults is that something is lacking in their experience of church. One-third said "church is boring" (31%) One-quarter of these young adults said that "faith is not relevant to my career or interests" (24%) or that "the Bible is not taught clearly or often enough" (23%). Sadly, one-fifth of these young adults who attended a church as a teenager said that "God seems missing from my experience of church" (20%).

A view held by many who turn away from Christ is that their parents are hypocrites. The reason: Children are often brought-up in households where, during the week, their parents live like the world and then, on Sunday mornings, they 'miraculously' turn into Christians. This type of discrepancy doesn't play well in the minds of thinking people and the young are always thinking and comparing.

When it comes to living Jesus out loud I often tell people that the concept is a bit like something my mother used to say: *"Kids learn by what a parent does more than by what they say. In other words, it doesn't do any good to tell a child... 'Do as I say, not as I do' because actions speak louder than words."*

I doubt my mom realized she was paraphrasing the Italian poet Giovanni Boccaccio but, as much as this quote has become 'cliché' in certain circles, it is a self-evident truth.

People really do 'learn by watching what you do' more than they 'learn by listening to what you say' because the way you live your life reflects what you truly believe more than any amount of words you use.

If for no other reason than the spiritual health of your family, I recommend that you try your very best to live the blessings Jesus has given you out loud. I promise, if you'll attempt to do this, God will bless your efforts.

It is my hope that this book will show you that by living Jesus out loud through projects that are both personally and culturally relative each and every person can be shown at least four things:

1) Christians have nothing to fear – because we've got God on our side.
2) We don't ignore the problems in the 'real world' because we're living like Christ Himself – by confronting the issues facing the world.
3) As the body of Christ, we can use music, movies and video games to challenge those we seek to touch with the love of Jesus.
4) The true Christian life is anything but boring. In fact, many of the outreaches you'll be introduced to aren't for the faint of heart and, because you'll be driven to do things that are out of your comfort zone, God will take the forefront of whatever it is you do.

With enough God-given ingenuity and imagination I can't imagine why we can't engage and answer all six reasons young people leave the church. The other four reasons are::

Reason #3 – Churches come across as antagonistic to science.
Reason #4 – Young Christians' church experiences related to sexuality are often simplistic, judgmental.
Reason #5 – They wrestle with the exclusive nature of Christianity.
Reason #6 – The church feels unfriendly to those who doubt.

In short, to paraphrase a popular ad, you'll learn why living Jesus out loud 'isn't your father's type of church.' For instance, while we would love to be able to shelter our children from the 'ways of the world' it simply isn't practical nor is it, I believe, wise. Instead, wisdom dictates that we present the ways of the world to our children in bite-sized pieces – pieces they can work through and digest so they aren't blindsided and their faith isn't hindered whenever they discover that a 'different world' awaits them outside of the safety of their home and church.

My son and daughter have been helping us minister to the homeless since they were around two years old. As such, they've seen and heard things that many children never encounter – such as people who are on drugs or alcohol and who do and say things that are inappropriate – at least from a Christian point-of-view. Obviously, my wife and I want to protect them from being negatively influenced by the world but, in our opinion, the best way to protect them is to allow them to become inoculated (build up a resistance) to attitudes and actions that are decidedly non-Christian because it allows their mother and I to more easily juxtapose the differences between the world we've been adopted into (Heaven) and the world in which we currently dwell.

Trust me, I am NOT suggesting that anyone 'inoculate' their children by allowing them to view pornography, listen to the death metal or secular rap music or by giving them permission to watch shows like 'Family Guy' or other inappropriate media. Instead, what I am suggesting is that, as Christians, we don't 'bury our heads in the sand' and simply pretend that the world doesn't exist outside of the four walls of our home and church. This type of xenophobia (the fear of that which is foreign) can be extremely damaging – not only to ourselves but to the cause of Christ. Remember, it is He who ate with, lived among and generally communed with sinners. If He is truly the One we are supposed to imitate then there's no reason whatsoever for us to hide behind anything other than His protection. If more of us took what is written in Psalm 27:1 as a promise to us, His children, we would be much more willing to strike out and overtake the world for Him.

"The LORD is my light and my salvation – whom shall I fear? The LORD is the stronghold of my life – of whom shall I be afraid?"

Unless we (Christians) are willing to LIVE as though Jesus is the MOST IMPORTANT PERSON in our lives then He won't be seen by others who know us as being important.

For the sake of our family, our friends, our community and, ultimately, for God, we should attempt to impress others with exemplary lives that are lived with Jesus as the centerpiece.

Take a moment and imagine how you would act if Jesus were around you 24 hours a day, 7 days a week, 365 days a year – walking beside us, riding in our cars with us, sitting at the desk next to us and looking over our shoulders when we're watching television, surfing the internet or reading books.

Now, imagine that Jesus could tell if you were only acting to 'get on His good side.' How would your behavior change if you truly believed that God Himself were living with you 100% of the time and that He knew your innermost thoughts – whether they were selfish or selfless; whether you truly were looking out for others or only yourself in the decisions you make; and whether or not the way you acted was really just a show or if it was part of who you were?

If you can imagine this, allow me to let you in on a not so secret truth: As His children, He IS with us 100% of the time – day and night, rain or shine, good days and bad. He is ALWAYS there.

If that freaks you out a little, write and tell me so I'll know I'm not the only one who is a little 'weirded out' by this truth.

While you're trying to wrap your mind around the concept of having the King of Kings, the Lord of Lords, your Creator and your Father with you ALWAYS, let me assure you that He is not hanging around with a big clipboard checking off things that you do wrong and right. As our Father, He is with me as I type this sentence and with you as you read it to serve as our Guide and our Instructor. When I use the terms 'Guide' and 'Instructor' I'm not referring to God as some metaphorical new age spirit being who is trying to help us find our own path. I'm telling you that GOD is present in your life and in mine and that He is willing, wanting and waiting for us to say '*Here I am Lord, send me. Do with me as you will.*'

Living Jesus Out Loud is about challenging yourself to live as though Jesus REALLY IS the King of Kings and the Lord of Lords in YOUR life.

I hope it inspires you to attempt that which no one is able to do through their own strength but is entirely possible with the help of the Holy Spirit.

Chapter 2

We Have Met the Enemy and He Is Us

I've chosen the title of this chapter (which comes from a cartoon strip character Pogo (circa 1970) created by author Walt Kelly) because it often seems (to pre-Christians) that the enemy of the Christian is our own spiritual kin. If we were able to step back and look 'in' from the 'outside' of Christianity I think we'd see why the world thinks this way about us.

The comments found in an article written by Ronald J. Sider titled, *"The Scandal of the Evangelical Conscience: Why don't Christians live what they preach?"* for Christianity Today illustrates exactly why living Jesus out loud for all the world to see is so important.

"Scandalous behavior is rapidly destroying American Christianity. By their daily activity, most "Christians" regularly commit treason. With their mouths they claim that Jesus is Lord, but with their actions they demonstrate allegiance to money, sex, and self-fulfillment." [Emphasis mine.]

The findings in numerous national polls conducted by highly respected pollsters like The Gallup Organization and The Barna Group are simply shocking. "Gallup and Barna," laments evangelical theologian Michael Horton, "*hand us survey after survey demonstrating that evangelical Christians are as likely to embrace lifestyles every bit as hedonistic, materialistic, self-centered, and sexually immoral as the world in general.*" Divorce is *more* common among "born-again" Christians than in the general American population. Only 6 percent of evangelicals tithe. White evangelicals are the *most* likely people to object to neighbors of another race. Josh McDowell has pointed out that the sexual promiscuity of evangelical youth is only a little less outrageous than that of their non-evangelical peers.

Alan Wolfe, famous contemporary scholar and director of the Boisi Center for Religion and American Public Life, has just published a penetrating study of American religious life. Evangelicals figure prominently in his book. His evaluation? Today's evangelicalism, Wolfe says, exhibits "*so strong a desire to copy the culture of hotel chains and popular music that it loses what religious distinctiveness it once had.*" Wolfe argues, "*The truth is there is increasingly little difference between an essentially secular activity like the popular entertainment industry and the bring-'em-in-at-any-cost efforts of evangelical megachurches.*"

It is not surprising that George Barna concludes, "*Every day, the church is becoming more like the world it allegedly seeks to change.*" We have very little time, he believes, to reverse these trends. African Christian and famous missions scholar Professor Lamin Sanneh told Christianity Today recently that "*the cultural captivity of Christianity in the West is nearly complete, and with the religion tamed, it is open season on the West's Christian heritage. I worry about a West without a moral center facing a politically resurgent Islam.*"

Our first concern, of course, must be internal integrity, not external danger. What a tragedy for evangelicals to declare proudly that personal conversion and new birth in Christ are at the center of their faith and then to defy biblical moral standards by living almost as sinfully as their pagan neighbors. [Emphasis mine.]

Graham Cyster, a Christian whom I know from South Africa, recently told me a painful story about a personal experience two decades ago when he was struggling against apartheid as a young South African evangelical. One night, he was smuggled into an underground Communist cell of young people fighting apartheid. *"Tell us about the gospel of Jesus Christ,"* they asked, half hoping for an alternative to the violent communist strategy they were embracing.

Graham gave a clear, powerful presentation of the gospel, showing how personal faith in Christ wonderfully transforms persons and creates one new body of believers where there is neither Jew nor Greek, male nor female, rich nor poor, black nor white. The youth were fascinated. One seventeen-year-old exclaimed, *"That is wonderful! Show me where I can see that happening."* Graham's face fell as he sadly responded that he could not think of anywhere South African Christians were truly living out the message of the gospel. *"Then the whole thing is a piece of sh– ,"* the youth angrily retorted. Within a month he left the country to join the armed struggle against apartheid – and eventually giving his life for his beliefs.

The young man was right. If Christians do not live what they preach, the whole thing is a farce. *"**American Christianity has largely failed since the middle of the twentieth century**,"* Barna concludes, *"**because Jesus' modern-day disciples do not act like Jesus**."* This scandalous behavior mocks Christ, undermines evangelism, and destroys Christian credibility." [Emphasis mine.]

The above article, in its entirety, can be found at:
www3.dbu.edu/jeanhumphreys/SocialPsych/evangelicalmind.htm

A Word of Wisdom: You ARE Going To Stumble and Fail – But It's Okay!

I can promise you at least one thing: Even if you are really, truly committed to living Jesus out loud in your life, you will fail from time to time. Guaranteed.

This doesn't mean that you have to be perfect before you try to live Jesus

31

out loud! I believe all Christians, regardless of where they are in their level of spiritual maturity, are called and commanded to live as though Christ is the center of their universe because He is!

My advice to you is simple: Don't try to fake anyone out – they'll eventually see through the charade and you'll end up embarrassed or, worse, impugning God's character.

The Bible warns that the world will not only judge *Christians* but they'll even go so far as to judge the *character of God* because of the way we act.

"And if you are confident that you [yourself] are a guide to the blind, a light to those who are in darkness, and [that You are] a corrector of the foolish, a teacher of the childish, having in the Law the embodiment of knowledge and truth – Well then, you who teach others, do you not teach yourself? While you teach against stealing, do you steal (take what does not really belong to you)? You who say not to commit adultery, do you commit adultery [are you unchaste in action or in thought]? You who abhor and loathe idols, do you rob temples [do you appropriate to your own use what is consecrated to God, thus robbing the sanctuary and doing sacrilege]? You who boast in the Law, do you dishonor God by breaking the Law [by stealthily infringing upon or carelessly neglecting or openly breaking it]? For, as it is written, The name of God is maligned and blasphemed among the Gentiles because of you!" Romans 2:19-24 (ABV)

This is an incredibly daunting warning for those who 'talk the talk' and yet don't 'walk the walk' of being a Christian. It may not have been Abraham Lincoln who actually said, *"You can fool some of the people all of the time, and all of the people some of the time, but you cannot fool all of the people all of the time,"* but, regardless of who did, it's true. Frankly, it's possible to fool even yourself into thinking something's true that is patently false. But, the one Person you CANNOT ever fool is God.

Again, Christians who attempt to fool others and get caught can cause people to not only stumble but to actually blaspheme God (i.e., they deny the being and perfections of God and speak evil about Him as well as His laws and the forms of worship instituted by Him – paraphrased from Gill's Commentary on Romans 2:24).

I can't think of anything worse than to be found guilty of leading someone away from the saving grace of God by my actions.

As you begin living Jesus out loud you may find that you become frustrated at your attempts to do so. While it may be hard to comprehend (especially if you're young in your faith), failing while trying is okay – in fact, it's more than okay... it's wonderful. The reason I say this is because if you ever find anyone who claims that they never fail you've probably also found someone who is deceived about what it means to live Jesus out loud or they don't really try to do so.

Along the same lines, when you're witnessing to others, don't worry all that much about what you say. Obviously, you should want to know what you're talking about before trying to witness to someone but that won't be a problem if you follow the command in
1 Timothy 2:15 – *"Be diligent to present yourself approved to God as a workman who does not need to be ashamed, accurately handling the word of truth."*

However, if you ever get into a situation where a person has backed you into a corner with questions, I'd suggest that you simply say: *"Look, I don't know the answer to the questions you're asking but I'm certain I can find someone who does. Until I have the chance to find the answers, let me tell you what Jesus has done for me in my life."*

I truly believe what I state in *Death, Heaven and Back – The True Story of One Man's Resurrection*:

"The next time you meet someone take the time to find out if they have a personal relationship with Jesus. If they don't, then tell them your story (the story of how you came to know Jesus), tell them my story or tell them of someone else you know who is living a victorious life in Jesus Christ. Regardless of whose story it is that you relate, tell them of Jesus and His great love for them. Don't worry that you'll not know what to say. If you're scared of witnessing to people, pray to God that the Holy Spirit will give you the right words to say. I'll make you a promise right here and right now... No matter what words you use, (even if you're the

33

best or the worst orator in history) it's not going to matter.

The reason is because you and I are simply extensions of God's grace (if you've personally accepted Him as your Savior) and, as such, all the pressure is off of us. No one who has ever lived, with the exception of God Himself, has ever brought anyone to God. Instead, He has always drawn people to Himself. What this means, to you and me, is that we can and should freely witness to everyone possible with the knowledge that regardless of how good or bad we do, salvation is His responsibility, not ours. But, when we do witness to people, we honor and glorify the One of whom we testify and we are rewarded for doing so. What a great 'job' we have as Christians. It's a win-win-win situation (they win, we win, and God wins)!" (Page 212)

Once, while I was on a plane, I overheard a conversation that reminded me of exactly why we need to sanctify Christ as Lord in our hearts, always being ready to make a defense to everyone who asks you to give an account for the hope that is in you, yet with gentleness (towards the listener) and reverence (towards God) – 1 Peter 3:15.

What you're about to read is a conversation between two gentlemen (Greg – a professing Christian and Dale – a professing agnostic). While what they said to one another is paraphrased to some degree, I assure you that I was taking notes as quickly as possible and the substance of what was said is accurate.

Chapter 3

The Kind of Witness We *Don't* Want To Be

You never know when the opportunity to be a witness for Jesus is going to arise. I mention this because while sitting in a plane waiting for a storm to clear, I overheard two guys sitting in front of me begin talking, rather loudly, about their experiences in Alcoholics Anonymous. It wasn't long until one of them (Dale) brought up the question of the 'higher power' mentioned in the 12-step program.

Dale openly questioned why so many people he met at the meetings he'd attended thought of the 'higher power' as being Jesus. Greg casually affirmed that he too believed that Jesus was the higher power in question. Incredulously, Dale asked, "*You mean you actually pray to Jesus as God?*" When Greg answered "*Yes*" the conversation began in earnest.

Greg told Dale he was raised Catholic and that he believed Jesus was God, the Bible was true, and we (mankind) had a responsibility to recognize this. Dale was full of questions about the Catholic faith specifically and about Christianity in general.

Patiently, Greg articulated his understanding of certain practices peculiar to Catholics as well as the doctrines of Christianity (Catholic and Protestant). Honestly, he did a great job. Even though I didn't (and don't) agree with everything he said as it pertained to the Catholic faith, he was, at the very least, being an honorable defender of Christianity and theism and he seemed to be getting through to Dale by answering the questions with 'gentleness and respect.'

Then... everything came crashing down.

Just as Dale seemed to be enjoying the conversation (he had asked really good questions and was responding very positively to the answers being given), the pilot announced that we'd be unable to take off for another half hour. Personally, while I wasn't looking forward to being delayed from getting home, I thought this was a terrific opportunity for Greg to continue ministering to Dale. Unfortunately, that didn't happen.

After the announcement, Greg called someone on his cell phone and said (paraphrased), "*We're in the (bleep) plane on the (bleep, bleep) runway because of a (major BLEEP) storm. We may not be able to get to Mississippi until (bleep) tomorrow. I hate this (bleep, bleep).*"

In case you haven't guessed, the 'bleeps' were foul language.

Immediately after Greg's phone call (and I mean the very next sentence), Dale said, "*Yeah, you know the AA manual has a section for agnostics. I read it and THAT WAS WRITTEN FOR ME exactly.*"

From that moment on Dale didn't ask another question about religion and Greg couldn't find a way to get the conversation going again. Why? Simple: He'd lost all credibility.

I'm sure that in Dale's mind Greg was a guy who 'talked the talk' but didn't 'walk the walk.'

This was a reminder to me that people really are watching those of us who claim to be Christians and that we are held to a higher level of accountability (as we should be) because we not only claim an allegiance to God but a relationship with Him.

Sobering, isn't it?

Chapter 4

Allowing People to Be Free In Jesus

While not meant to be strictly logically cohesive, the following three points sum up the emphasis of this chapter.

- God is love.
- Love is freedom.
- God's love equals freedom.

When Jesus came to the world He created, He did so without much fanfare. Spiritual impact withstanding, Jesus' birth is considered by much of modern academia to be something of a non-event historically. Yet, some 2,000 years later the world stands divided into three major sects :

- Those who believe Jesus truly lived but who claim there's not enough evidence to show that Jesus, as the Christ, was born into this world.

- Those who believe Jesus never existed and, therefore, did not come as God, Messiah or Savior.

- Those who believe that Jesus came as God, Messiah and Savior and accept Him as such.

Regardless of whether one considers Jesus a mythological figurehead or the real, transcendent and manifested God of the world, no one argues that He is a major focal point of history. It has been said that His birth divided history.

In his poem, *One Solitary Life*, Dr. James Allen states of Jesus:

"*...all the armies that have ever marched, all the navies that have ever sailed, all the parliaments that have ever sat, all the kings that ever reigned put together, have not affected the life of mankind on earth as powerfully as that one solitary life.*"

While it's easy to understand, based on the human desire to serve a person or an ideal greater than themselves, how Jesus may have impacted the generation living when He walked on the earth (much like Siddhārtha Gautama Buddha (Buddha) or Vernon Wayne Howell (better known as David Koresh of the Branch Davidians) or even President Barack Obama), no one has so affected the world or effected change in the same more than Jesus.

While some scholars may disagree whether Jesus or Mohammed is the 'king' of conversion, no one denies that the two figureheads (Jesus = Christianity; Mohammed = Islam) converted their followers in quite different manners. Despite the fact that some so-called devotees of both religions have gone 'against the grain' (some calling themselves Christians have 'converted' people through forceful methods while others calling themselves Muslim have 'converted' people through peaceful methods), historically there is a world of difference between the two.

On the whole, Islam has gained so-called converts through the threat of subjugation, heavy taxation and even the threat of death. I use the term 'so-called converts' because it's exceedingly rare for a sane person to experience a true conversion (the acceptance of all the tenets of a belief system) while under duress. It has been my experience that Dale

Carnegie was correct when he said, *"Those convinced against their will are of the same opinion still."* Conversely, Christianity has gained true converts through liberation, the demonstration of Christ's love and helping people live better lives.

Speaking prophetically of Himself and His arrival into the world, Jesus stated, in Matthew 10:34, *"Do not think that I came to bring peace on earth. I did not come to bring peace but a sword. For I have come to 'set a man against his father, a daughter against her mother, and a daughter-in-law against her mother-in-law'; and 'a man's enemies will be those of his own household.'"*

The recommendation not to speak about politics or religion if one wants to keep the peace at a family gathering is anecdotal proof that most people consider Jesus' prophecy to be true – even if they don't accept Him as being God.

As an aside, before someone assumes Jesus was talking about a literal sword and tries to make a comparison between Christianity and Islam, one should note that the stories He told would have been recognized immediately by His Jewish listeners as featuring God as the ultimate agent of *reconciliation*.

A prime example is the story of the Prodigal Son (which could also be titled, 'A Father's Unceasing Love.') in Luke 11. The Lord tells of a young child who falls into the traps of greed and egocentric thinking. Instead of waiting for his father to give him his inheritance, the young man demands that he be given his share of the same immediately.

Upon receiving his inheritance the young man leaves his home and goes into the world where he quickly squanders the wealth he has been afforded from the work of his father. Before long he becomes destitute and determines to return home and beg his father for a job as a menial slave – a major step-up from competing with pigs for 'choice bits' of slop.

Jesus tells us that even while the son was far from his former household his father sees him and runs to meet him. Upon reaching his son the father hugs the child and kisses him. The son confesses his sin against

41

his father and denies that he is even worthy of being called the man's son.

The father, who is implicitly understood to have already apprehended his child's repentance (the son made the choice to return to his first love – his family), in his sheer delight to have his son return to him, orders servants to dress him in the best clothes and for a feast to be thrown in order to celebrate the return of the young man. In explaining his excitement to his oldest son (who is far from delighted about his brother being welcomed back in such a grandiose fashion) the father states that the older sibling has lost nothing from his brother returning but, instead, has inherited a greater thing than all the wealth of the father. Namely, the father tells the older brother *"My son you are always with me, and everything I have is yours. But we had to celebrate and be glad, because this brother of yours was dead and is alive again; he was lost and is found."*

This sounds remarkably parallel to Matthew 18:12 in which we're told that *"If a man owns a hundred sheep, and one of them wanders away, will he not leave the ninety-nine on the hills and go to look for the one that wandered off? And if he finds it, truly I tell you, he is happier about that one sheep than about the ninety-nine that did not wander off."*

The Jewish audience to whom Jesus was speaking would have instantly recognized that He was speaking about the nation of Israel (who had long since turned from their First Love (God) and had squandered their wealth but who, if they returned to Him, would be loved and cherish as if they'd never left. Of course, more generally, Jesus was speaking (in both stories) about individuals 'who were lost but then found.'

In both parables it should be noted that *it is the father (shepherd)* who goes out to meet and bring home the one who is lost.

Every story told to us in the Bible of Jesus or His Father 'drawing to,' 'finding,' or 'not losing' people (that I recall) is a story of reconciliation through love rather than force.

I believe the over-arching theme (metanarrative) of the Bible is about relationship – God's relationship to us, our relationship to Him and our relationship with others.

The Bible is clear that this over-arching theme wouldn't have been possible without Him first instituting the ultimate reconciliation process towards those He loves (mankind) by becoming a man, living among us, dying for us because we had sinned against Him and rising from the grave to prove He has power over both life and death.

It is this 'Good News' that we, as His children, have been called to spread throughout the world to any and all who will listen. Of course, there are many different ways to convey (evangelize) the messages of this metanarrative including:

1. Interpersonally (Seeking an individual relationship)
2. Confrontationally (Using direct questions)
3. Referentially (Utilizing testimonials)
4. Intellectually (Applying logic and reason)
5. Propositionally (Inviting others to explore for themselves)
6. Demonstrably (Showing through actions)

Depending on your specific personality you may be more or less drawn to one type of evangelization method. Personally, I've found people respond better and quicker to the Gospel message when I've used the first, third and especially the sixth type of evangelization.

That being said, I was initially drawn to review the claims of the Bible via a combination of confrontational, intellectual and propositional evangelization. However, if it weren't for the fact that the man who confronted me had first engendered an interpersonal relationship with me by showing, through his actions, that his beliefs were achievable, I wouldn't have been willing to give any credence to his intellectual challenge. Yet, because he was a living testimony of 'love in action,' I was drawn to God through his insistence that I read the Bible.

Once I had given my life fully to Christ I became, in a word, *free*. I believe if all Christians realized that freedom in Christ was the ultimate goal for everyone, evangelizing would become a party!

If we paraphrase St. Augustine and advise those we meet to "*Love God with all your heart, soul, strength and mind and then live in any manner that pleases you*" and they heed this suggestion they will find a freedom that is extremely liberating.

It's not liberating because they are free to live without restraint but *because of the restraints placed on us by the suggestion.*

Indeed, living out the first instruction (to love God completely) would dictate how we followed the second (to live in any manner that pleases you) so that we'd never want to lead a lifestyle that would do anything that displeases Him. Jesus sums up how He wants us to live in John 15:9-17 (paraphrased): 'If you love Me, you will obey Me and what I want you to do is to love others.'

For a Christian, Jesus is the ultimate expression of truth, truth is the ultimate expression of freedom and freedom (through and because of God) is the ultimate expression of love.

Conversely, the spirit of the Anti-Christ (either a substitution for Christ or that which is against Christ) is the ultimate expression of lies, lies are the ultimate expression of bondage and bondage is the ultimate expression of hate.

Put another way, love has self-limiting boundaries whereas hate is limited only when it encounters love. Love liberates and gives us sight whereas hate binds and blinds us. Love helps us overcome adversity; hate makes us succumb to adversity.

The first chorus of Brandon Heath's song, *Give Me Your Eyes*, tells the story of someone begging to see people the way God sees them:

"Give me your eyes for just one second
Give me your eyes so I can see
Everything that I keep missing
Give me your love for humanity
Give me your arms for the broken hearted
Ones that are far beyond my reach.
Give me your heart for the ones forgotten

Give me your eyes so I can see."

The ending of the second chorus of the song concludes:

I want a second glance
So give me a second chance
To see the way You see people all along.

I'm convinced this is a prayer God is more than willing to answer. While it is Christians who should lead the battle cry of *'I am second'* rather than *'Me first,'* so many of us, like our pre-Christian counterparts, are too self-centered to truly pray that God would allow us to see others the way He sees them.

As the rest of this book concerns itself with outreach ministries, I'd like to share some advice before going further.

Those who want to reach out to others should be given massive amounts of freedom to share the love of Jesus in a manner that best suits their personality. I've found that when freedom is allowed to be exercised, everyone is surprised at the ingenuity of those whom He allows to work for Him.

Often, when freedom is exercised, the word 'unconventional' best describes what takes place under the banner of ministry – offering a homeless person the use of your shower, helping a prostitute leave his/her lifestyle, cleaning toilets at a neighborhood gas station or, perhaps, massaging the feet of strippers.

Regardless of how the Lord manifests His love for others, allowing people the freedom to do that which He calls them will result in magnificent results.

Chapter 5

Learn To Rely On God To Help You In Your Witness For Him

I had to learn how to rely on God to help me be an effective witness for Him the hard way. The reason is because I studied with the Jehovah's Witnesses (the group of people who proselytize for the Watchtower Bible and Tract Organization) for a bit more than three years prior to giving my life to Jesus.

I was 'ripe for the picking' because I had almost zero religious instruction in my childhood. In fact, about the only thing we prayed for on a regular basis was that my father (who was a violent alcoholic) wouldn't hurt one of us. Plus, I was genuinely seeking answers about life and God. The Jehovah's Witness who met me seemed to embody what I thought Christians were supposed to be: kind, considerate, thoughtful, concerned about my spiritual well-being, friendly and studious – especially as it concerned the Bible.

Like most, I began studying the Bible – which really meant we studied what the Watchtower and Awake magazines had to say about the Bible – at my home and this eventually led to my attending a Kingdom Hall. I give thanks to Jehovah that He allowed me to see serious contradictions in the study materials from which I was being taught because they caused me to begin questioning those who were teaching me.

Over and over I was told that the answer to the questions I brought up concerning the Biblical texts could be found in the original Koine Greek language the New Testament was translated from. I was told that the study materials we read from were faithfully transmitting the correct ideas, concepts and definitions. Ironically, had it not been for the study materials that so often dismissed other translations, I may not have noticed blatant contradictions in the materials we were being taught from.

In my pursuit of the truth, I decided to begin an informal study of the Kione Greek language. While I would grant that my study wasn't professionally supervised (I didn't go to school but, rather, choose to seek out study materials own my own – most of which were published by the Zondervan publishing company), after a bit more than two years of study I was able to read, fairly fluently, Biblical Greek and the texts found in the Kingdom Interlinear Translation (KIT) and the Emphatic Diaglott (ED) – both published by the Watchtower Bible and Tract Society WTBTS in the early 1980's.

During my studies I read very few materials that were consider adulterated by the WTBTS and none which were written by 'apostates' (those who had left the Jehovah's Witnesses either voluntarily or who had been disfellowshipped (excommunicated). In fact, during the two years I was formulating and asking questions, I faithfully went to weekly study groups and even began going door to door to proselytize people in hopes that they would accept Jehovah as the one true God.

However, as I grew more knowledgeable about the languages in which the New Testament had been written, I grew more discontented with the pat answers that were given and accepted. That the answers were accepted, without question, by those I considered much more knowledgeable than me disturbed me greatly.

Finally, during a Wednesday service, after we'd heard a district overseer teaching on apostasy and the woes of the current world, I began to be very vocal about some questions I had. I figured that the district overseer (who, by the way, has since become a true Christian and is therefore considered an apostate by the WTBTS) would be able to answer my questions from a mature standpoint.

While I can't remember the exact question I began with I think it had something to do with the way Jesus was supposedly placed on a stake (stauros) and the fact that the Bible (in both English and Greek) noted that nails (plural) were used to hold His hands on the stake whereas in every picture I'd ever seen published by the WTBTS Jesus' hands were shown placed together in such a way that, like His feet, only one nail (singular) would have been used to hold them (both His hands and feet) to the stake. From there I went on to inquire as to why it was that the Bible (NWT and ED) quoted Jesus as saying, in John 2:18-21 that He (Jesus) would raise Himself from the grave?

New World Translation: *"Therefore, in answer, the Jews said to him: "What sign have you to show us, since you are doing these things?" In answer Jesus said to them: "Break down this temple, and in three days **I will raise it up**." Therefore the Jews said: "This temple was built in forty-six years, and will you raise it up in three days?" But he was talking about the temple of **his body**."* [Emphasis mine.]

Emphatic Diaglott: *"Then the Jews answered and said to him, "What sign dost thou show us, why thou doest these things?" Jesus answered and said to them, "Destroy this TEMPLE, and in Three Days **I will raise it**." Then the Jews said, "Forty and Six Years has this TEMPLE been in building and wilt thou erect it in Three Days?" But he spoke of the TEMPLE of **his BODY**."* [Emphasis mine.]

I explained that I was concerned with the rendering of the text because it seemed to imply, at the very least, a contradiction of one of three WTBTS teachings and perhaps all three:

1. That Jesus, who was obviously dead at the time of His crucifixion, somehow had the ability to raise Himself from the grave even though I had been taught, repeatedly, that Jehovah God ALONE had raised Him.

2. That soul sleep (a very important doctrine espoused by the WTBTS) wasn't real since it would be obvious that if a person could raise their own body from the dead that they would have to be aware that they had died.

3. That either Jesus was lying or someone else was wrong about the body that was raised from death. I'd been taught for years that once Jesus, the man, had died that Jehovah God had recreated a body for Michael the Archangel (the being who was supposedly the pre-incarnate Christ) and that the original body was gone forever. However, this verse seemed to contradict that view. So, either Jesus lied or was wrong about being able to raise His own body or Jehovah God lied to us by presenting a duplicate Jesus (not the *same* Jesus) to the disciples or, somehow, what I'd been taught for the past 3 years was horribly in error.

While I asked these questions with all humility (though with a demand for an answer) they ended up being the last three in-depth questions I ever got to ask at a Kingdom Hall.

The district overseer once again answered (paraphrased), "*Lonnie, you'd understand the intricacies of this passage if you could read the original Greek.*" When I asked him if he could read the original Greek he said "*No.*" I then told him that I could and proceeded to do so.

With every eye on he and I (about ten folks had gathered around us by this time), he stared at me blankly for a few moments and then motioned for me to follow him.

We eventually stopped by the front door of the Kingdom Hall and I was told (paraphrased): "*Lonnie, you've been 'in the light' for some time now. I don't know why it is you haven't committed yourself fully to Jehovah God and been baptized but, it seems to me that you've been studying apostate literature. Your questions are causing many here to question the truth that Jehovah God has revealed to them so I'd like to ask you to leave and not return until you are ready to come under the tutelage of an elder who will then guide you back into the light.*"

He opened the door, motioned for me to leave and that was that. I was out.

I remember standing outside the Kingdom Hall door completely stunned. These people were the only 'Christians' I knew and yet they'd just kicked me out of their community.

I left with such distaste for anything remotely resembling Christianity that it would be difficult for me to adequately explain. I decided that if Jehovah would allow this to happen I didn't need Him. Thankfully, He hadn't given up on me.

To make a long story shorter (I'll be explaining what brought me back to God later in this book), I eventually gave my life to Jesus and became a true student of His Word.

Now that you have some background information on my religious background, I'll get to the point of this chapter.

The Comma That Saves

I'd been a Christian for approximately two years when Dave approached me and began asking me questions about the Jehovah's Witnesses. It turned out that the same person who had introduced me to the organization had been proselytizing Dave's wife and she was considering becoming one of Jehovah's baptized witnesses. While I really, truly loved

Diane, the Jehovah's Witness who'd originally talked to me about her religion and who was now speaking to Jordan, I also knew she was following (and leading Jordan and Dave) down a path that wasn't Godly at all. Dave asked me if I'd mind coming over to his home to discuss some of the issues that Diane and I disagreed about. I jumped at the chance.

The night I arrived at Dave's and Jordan's home I was, metaphorically, loaded for bear. It took me three trips to my car to get everything I'd brought for the debate. I had the New World Translation, the Emphatic Diaglott, the Kingdom Interlinear Translation of the Greek Scriptures, a King James Version Bible, a New International Version Bible and a New American Standard Bible along with Greek and Hebrew Lexicons, New and Old Testament Dictionaries and approximately 500 photocopied sheets of WTBTS documents dating back to the late 1800's.

In other words, I was prepared to debate and *I was going to win*!

[At this point I think it's only fair to note that in preparing for what I considered was going to be a battle royal – me against a satanic organization – I hadn't taken the time to truly pray for God to show-up and for Him to be glorified. Instead, this debate was all about me and what I had learned. In other words, I went to the debate with an ego that was so inflated it blinded me to the fact that God loved everyone who was going to be participating in studying His Word.]

As we began debating, it became clear that Diane was woefully unprepared for the level or types of arguments I was bringing to the discussion. At first she seemed perplexed over the fact that I was so forceful in disagreeing with the beliefs she knew I'd been taught years before. But, after about an hour, her bewilderment turned into outright defiance and we began to debate in earnest.

Honestly, I was thrilled to have the chance to 'put Diane in her place' and I did my very best to do so. I was keeping score mentally and, after we'd gone through around fifteen doctrinal issues, I figured that I was winning 15-0 or, at the very least, 14-1.

I was whipping out Scriptures as fast as she was and introducing documents as if I were an attorney and my life depended on this one debate. Two hours into the debate I noticed that Jordan had almost completely tuned out. She was only half-listening to what we were saying. Dave, on the other hand, was still fully connected. That was enough of an audience for me. I turned the intensity up a notch by beginning to talk about the false prophecies that had been preached by the WTBTS for years that had never come about. Somehow, this led to our talking about the prophecy of Jesus' resurrection and then soul sleep. I don't remember how we got around to the verse but, we ended up discussing Luke 23:43. This verse reads differently depending on whether you read it from the New World Translation or ANY standard English translation. The difference, as you can see for yourself below, is where the comma is placed in the verse.

"And He said to him, "Truly I say to **you, today** *you shall be with Me in Paradise.""* (NASB) [Emphasis mine.]

"And he said to him: "Truly *I tell you* **today, you** *will be with me in Paradise.""* (NWT) [Emphasis mine.]

"And he said to him, *"Indeed I say to* **thee, This day** *thou shalt be with me in PARADISE.""* (ED) [Emphasis mine.]

Diane and I talked about this verse at length. The main thrust of her argument was that the comma had been placed after the word 'today' because those who translated the NWT knew Jesus wasn't talking about an event that was going to take place 'that very day' (the WTBTS teaches the unbiblical and indefensible doctrine of soul sleep). I was quick to point out that if one were to study how the phrase 'Truly I say to you' (Greek: amen soi lego) is used, you'd find it occurs 74 times in the Gospels and is, without exception, used as an introductory expression. I also pointed out that in 73 out of the 74 times the phrase occurs even the New World Translation places a break (such as a comma) AFTER the phrase, 'Truly I tell you.' The ONLY exception to this, in the NWT, is Luke 23:43.

I argued that the reason for this discrepancy was because IF they were to place a break before the word 'today' in Luke 23:43 it would ultimately destroy the eschatology (the study of end times) they teach. I then noted that even in the Emphatic Diaglott the translator (Benjamin Wilson) placed the comma before the phrase 'This day.' After fifteen minutes of looking up the other 73 occurrences of the phrase (which I had conveniently printed out from the NWT), Diane quickly changed the subject and I went right along with her.

Ten minutes after leaving the subject of soul sleep, Diane and I were in a deep argument about the Trinity and Dave interrupted us (for the first time in over two hours).

Even as Diane and I were debating, I'd noticed that he'd been flipping through the various Bibles I had brought as well as others he had in his own home. His search culminated in him asking, "*I have a question about the comma in Luke 23:43. Why is it that it's placed before the word 'today' in every other Bible except the New World Translation?*"

Once again Diane and I explained the reasons for the change and, once again, I thought that I'd handily won the discussion. Diane, apparently not wanting to explore the reasons for the differences in the translations, hurriedly moved onto another subject. But, Dave just wouldn't leave Luke 23:43 alone and, over the course of the next thirty minutes, he brought us back to it twice more.

Frankly, was getting annoyed at Dave. We'd already explained why the WTBTS had decided to place the comma where they did in Luke 23:43 three times. I thought to myself, "*Man, it's just a comma. Get over it. I mean, really, we're talking about the Trinity which is MUCH more important than a comma.*"

To make a long story shorter, after three hours of intense debate, we decided to call it a night. I packed up all my materials (minus most of the photocopied pages from the WTBTS' articles – which I left for Dave and Jordan to go over at their leisure), gave all them a hug and left. I was convinced that I had done an exemplary work for God and had won the vast majority of points Diane and I had discussed. All-in-all, I was extremely proud of my knowledge and ability to present the same.

Fast forward two months.

Dave and I worked for the same company and I was in one of several breakrooms when he found me. He came to me, shook my hand and, with a big smile on his face, told me, "*Jordan and I have stopped going to the Kingdom Hall and we've both committed our lives to Jesus Christ Who we now know is God.*"

I remember feeling a swell of pride in my chest and, as I sat back in my chair I asked him, "*So, what was it that made you change your mind?*"

I was fully anticipating having my ego massaged. I waited for Dave to wax poetically about my oratory and debating skills and for him to thank me for teaching he and his wife what the Bible truly said.

Proverbs 16:18 states, emphatically, that "*Pride goes before destruction, a haughty spirit before a fall.*" Until that day I had no idea that the 'destruction' or the 'fall' could happen to one who sincerely believed he or she was doing God's work.

Dave answered, "***It was that comma in Luke 23:43.*** *I just couldn't get past it so I started looking at everything else the Watchtower had written and found that a lot of things were like that comma.*" [Emphasis mine.]

The comma?

A comma had driven two people to the cross of Jesus Christ and His love?

A comma... *seriously?*

I couldn't believe Dave didn't mention anything at all about my skillful dissection of the WTBTS' theology or my expertise in Scripture. Instead, it was a comma... a lowly, simple, small, tiny mark in a Bible with some

770,000 words that had been used by God to take this husband and wife from pre-Christians to Christians; from those who were destined to spend eternity in Hell to those who will be beside me and all other brothers- and sisters-in-Christ in Heaven forever and ever.

Dave left the breakroom soon after his comments and, as I sat by myself, the Holy Spirit convicted me of my pride by bringing to mind Mark 5:18 which tells us: *"For truly I say to you, until heaven and earth pass away, not the smallest letter or stroke shall pass from the Law until all is accomplished."*

Interestingly enough, Mark 5:18 was one of the Scriptures I'd brought up in our debate concerning the correct placement of the comma in Luke 23:43.

I broke down in tears when I realized that I had nothing to do with the conversion experienced by Dave and Jordan. The tears I wept were bitter and sweet… bitter because I realized I had embarrassed myself before Almighty God by not relying on Him to speak through me and sweet because, from that day on, I knew I'd never forget the story of 'The Comma That Saves.'

As I said at the beginning of the chapter, I learned the hard way how to rely on God to help me be an effective witness for Him. Fortunately, I'm a fairly sharp student and once the lesson was taught I never forgot it.

With this being said, I'd like to tell you about another conversion story I was allowed to be part of simply because I did what the Lord told me to do and no more.

Chapter 6

Jose, a Former Homosexual, Turns His Life Over to Jesus

Jose and I met during one of the hospital visitations I routinely make. Frankly, I didn't remember meeting him (it's one of the things I have to cope with since I suffer from short-term memory loss) but, fortunately, he remembered meeting me and thankfully, as Jose tells the story, I helped him meet Jesus. In actuality, God simply allowed me to be there when He introduced Himself to Jose.

[Note: With Jose's permission I've restructured the original letter he sent to me so it reads less like a letter written directly to me and more like prose. Also, for the sake of propriety, I've taken out a few of the more illicit references Jose made in his letter as it relates to his former lifestyle.] The letter read...

"Pastor Lonnie and I met when he came to see Jon, a friend of mine. I remember seeing a short, little white guy I'd never met coming into Jon's hospital room and thinking '*Who is this guy?*'

Anne, Jon's fiancée, introduced him as Pastor Lonnie and I thought, '*Oh man, just what I need… a Bible-thumper.*'

At the time I felt justified in my attitude but, not long after I got to know Lonnie, I realized that I was more worried about what a minister was going to say to me than I was about Jon's health. In other words, I realized that I was very self-centered. But, I'm getting ahead of the story.

I was the first person Anne introduced to Pastor Lonnie and I expected him to be repulsed by all the piercings I had (my nose, eyebrow and lips all had piercings at the time and I was very proud of them). Not only that but I was a gay man and I'd never tried to hide that fact from anyone – including my uncle, Antonio, who is also a pastor. Antonio and I had had a lot of conversations over the past fifteen years concerning my homosexuality. Actually, they were more shouting matches rather than conversations.

Antonio, who worked with the underprivileged in our community, could never bring himself to look at me with anything except disgust. He told me homosexuality was an abomination to God and he seemed to never be able to see past the fact I was gay to also see I was his nephew and a person – to me it seemed I was always "*Jose, my gay nephew*" rather than just "*Jose, my nephew.*"

Anyway, since I was trying to be respectful for the sake of my friends, I stuck my hand out to shake Lonnie's. But, unexpectedly, Lonnie bypassed my hand and gave me a hug!! I couldn't believe it. To say that I was shocked would be an understatement. No one EVER hugged me – not even my own father and mother! I can't tell you how long it's been since anyone has hugged me. Even the lovers I've had during my life have rarely been able to get close enough to me to actually give me a hug like Pastor Lonnie did. It seems that I was the one who was shaken up, not him.

As soon as he'd hugged everyone in the room, Anne told us that Lonnie had died, gone to Heaven and came back. I remember rolling my eyes and deciding it was time for me to leave. So, as soon as he bowed his head to pray, I quickly and quietly left the room.

Twenty minutes later I'd made my way to the hospital cafeteria and was having cup of tea when guess who walks in – Pastor Lonnie! Even though I'd slunk down in the booth I was sitting in and averted my eyes from his direction in an attempt to hide, I felt a quick pat on my shoulder as he walked by and heard him say, "*Hey, Jose, mind if I join you for a minute or two?*" I politely nodded 'Yes' but, inwardly, I dreaded having to spend any time at all with a minister.

Quicker than I would have liked, Lonnie had returned from getting a cold drink and was back at the booth, sitting directly in front of me.

I was taken aback by the fact he seemed to smile a lot and when he talked to me it wasn't all 'Bible-this' and 'Bible-that' but, instead, he engaged me in a real conversation. He asked how long I'd known Jon and Anne (6 years), whether or not I was from the area (No) and then he did something I didn't expect at all… he asked me how long I'd been gay!! I couldn't believe he was that bold. When I told him 'all my life' I was expecting him to start preaching to me but all he did was nod his head and stop talking. We must have set there for about five minutes with him just smiling at me. Every now and again he would take a sip from his cup but other than this he didn't try to engage me further. The smile never left his face. It was a little annoying and very unsettling.

Finally, I couldn't take it any more so I asked, very defensively, "*So, do you or your 'god'* (I emphasized the word as I said it) *have a problem with me being gay?*" Still smiling he said, "*Yes. But, we're both certain you can change.*" That ticked me off. I rose up to my fullest height and, even though we were still sitting, I was at least a foot taller than him (he's quite short) and I loudly asked, "*So, you're both certain that I can change are you? Well, why in Hell should I want to change?*"

I remember that once I'd said this, Pastor Lonnie slowly stopped smiling, looked down at the table as if he were trying to see through it and then he looked back at me with a concerned look on his face and said, "*Not because of Hell. Heaven's the reason God and I want you to change."* For a long moment he was quiet and I was so shocked at the sincerity in his voice that I didn't say anything either. Then he asked, *"Do you mind if I tell you my story?"* Since I didn't say 'No' he began to tell me about his childhood, his teen years and his early adulthood.

To my utter surprise, Lonnie was very open and honest. He talked to me as if I were his friend instead of someone he'd just met. He talked about all the ways he used to sin and some of the ways he still did and then he told me about his death, his trip to Heaven and what he's been doing since coming back.

Then, Lonnie told me something no other 'Christian' had ever done – at least not in the way he did. He said, *"You already know that homosexuality is considered to be wrong by God. But, did you know that ANY form of sex outside of marriage is considered a sin? The Bible tells us that ANY sin you and I commit are all condemnable acts in the eyes of God because all of them will send us to Hell. Did you know that God is fair enough that He'll punish a straight man for having consensual sex with a straight woman as much as He'll punish a gay man or a gay woman for having sex outside of marriage?"*

Honestly, I never knew that the Bible said that.

Pastor Lonnie went on and told me exactly what sin is and that no one who sins goes to Heaven unless their sins are forgiven. Then he told me God was so loving that He came to earth as a human, lived a perfect life and died in MY place so I wouldn't have to spend eternity without Him! Then Lonnie did something no straight man has EVER done for me… he told me he LOVED me.

When he told me this I didn't detect any sarcasm or pity in his voice. What I did feel was that this man – a man who hadn't known me an hour before – really did love me. But, Lonnie also said that Jesus loved me more than he did and, regardless of what I'd done in the past, He'd forgive me and would adopt me into His family.

Then, he told me something I didn't want to hear… Pastor Lonnie told me that in order to be forgiven by God I'd have to agree that being gay was wrong in His eyes, turn away from my gay lifestyle and ask Jesus to forgive me for this sin and all the other ways I'd done wrong. Lonnie told me he believed Jesus loved me as much as anyone else so that if I was sincere in turning away from being gay (something I didn't think was possible at the time) God would give me the strength and the resources I needed to stay away from my homosexual ways. With not much more than that and another quick hug, he left.

I sat in the booth for a long while before I noticed that he'd left a business card with his name, number and the website for 99 for 1 Ministries – **www.99for1ministries.com**. I put the card in my pocket and promptly forgot about it – *until Saturday night.*

Saturday night was a turning point in my life. I'd just gotten home from a date and found that I was extremely depressed. I didn't know why I was depressed. My date had gone very well. I'd not had anything to drink (I don't ever do drugs) and the guy I had seen that evening had even purchased me a gift. So, there was no reason for me to be sad. But, I was sad... amazingly sad.

As I sat alone in my home, what Pastor Lonnie had told me about his going to Heaven, seeing people he knew in Hell and the reason they were there – because they'd not accepted Christ as God and their Savior – kept running through my head. I kept remembering that this man had looked at me with love rather than contempt and disgust. I wanted to know how it was someone who had just met me could truly love someone so distinctly different than he was. I wondered how it was a straight man could feel comfortable enough with me, an obviously homosexual man, to not only engage me in such intimate conversation but could also hug me as if I were part of his own family?

To make a long story short, on Saturday night I began to think about what Pastor Lonnie had said and how he'd accepted me right where I was and that if Jesus was someone he thought highly of I might want to consider Him too. So, I got on the computer, looked up his ministries' website and from there I began searching for myself who God is.

Following a few of the links that are on 99 for 1 Ministries' site I found a LOT of information on Jesus, His Father and the Holy Spirit. While what I learned during the course of just a few hours was a bit confusing, I came to understand that The Father, The Son and The Holy Spirit are the same God and that I'm loved by Him. I don't pretend to understand how that works but I know as I keep studying and asking questions I'll get a better understanding. Anyway...

At about 3 a.m. I began crying and I asked Jesus into my heart. I told him I knew being gay was wrong, that I wanted to change and I wanted Him to be proud of me. Afterwards, I felt cleaner than I EVER had. I'd known, for years upon years, even when I was engaging in homosexual acts that felt good, in the back of my mind, something was wrong – I just never knew what it was.

Now, today, I've been 'clean' for months. What I mean is that I've not even had a sexual thought about a man (or a woman either). Lonnie says that one of these days I may have an urge to see men again but he also tells me if I remember who Christ is in my life and I 'run' from the urge God will give me the strength to resist the urge.

Anyhow, on that Saturday night I became a Christian.

My commitment to Jesus has changed my entire life. I've distanced myself from many of my old friends (most of whom were living a homosexual lifestyle) by actually moving from the city in which I used to live. I've even had 'words' with my Uncle Antonio – who now understands why it is he wasn't ever able to get past my defenses. Most importantly, I now understand what the old saying about 'people not caring how much you know until they know how much you care' really means. Pastor Lonnie showed me a side of Christ I'd never seen before the day I'd met him.

Since becoming a Christian, Pastor Lonnie and has introduced me to a group of Christians who specialize in helping men and women who, like me, want to beat the gay lifestyle. He also suggested a church I should look into and when I did (I admit I was scared to death that no one would want me to be in their building with them), I was happily surprised. Not only did they accept me (I still had spiky hair, a tattoo and all the piercings), they seemed genuinely happy I was there. The Christians I've met in my church seem truly committed to helping me show those I've introduced to Jesus who were living in sin (not necessarily homosexuality) the love of Jesus.

Since becoming a member of the family of Christ I've taken out every piercing I had because they represented the 'old' me and I've gotten a haircut – no one told me to do any of this, I just feel better this way. I love Jesus and I know He loves me and YOU!"

As an addendum to Jose's story, I'm happy to announce that after two years of being a truly committed Christian, God put a lady in his life. Since that time they've gone from being good friends to being engaged to be married. Sheila and Jose have begun pre-marital counseling at the church they attend and are planning to be wed in early 2013.

The purpose of my including this testimony is to show you that, more often than you might think, it's not what you say but what you do when you're witnessing that makes an impact on the heart of those to whom you are ministering.

Chapter 7

Focus On Showing the Love of Christ!

For years I was borderline obsessed with the study of prophecy. I don't believe there's anything wrong with studying prophecy or any other aspect of the Word of God. But, I do know it's possible to become distracted by almost anything we obsess over. For example, I've met many Christians who are so focused on a particular facet of the Christian life (Bible study, evangelism, marital counseling, community action, etc.) that they completely, although unwittingly, alienate those who are not 'all ears' towards their particular bent. Note that I said 'unwittingly.' I chose this word because I don't believe that any Christian I've ever met, whose passion is pure, sets out to push away anyone (Christian or pre-Christian). Nevertheless, without a sharp, discerning spirit, it happens all the time.

It's been said that if we were to look at a person's bank statements we'd see where their heart is. While I agree with this principle in general, I think such an observation is naïve because it spotlights only a single portion of a life. Instead, I believe if we observe a persons overall habits (what they talk about, concentrate on, spend their money and time on, etc.) we'd come closer to discovering the desire of their hearts.

In my case, I was consumed with the study of prophecy yet I had a true desire to bring people to Christ. As such, I spent my money and time preaching, teaching and contending for the souls I encountered. Still, by focusing almost entirely on one aspect of the Bible (prophecy), I inadvertently alienated those who had zero interest in the subject I had chosen to focus on. As I matured, I realized (or was shown) the mistakes of my method of evangelism. But, as I've already stated, I don't think we should worry all that much about what we say when presenting God to others because, as long as we do it in love, He will reward our presentation. I most certainly saw His hand on my method of ministry because a lot of people who studied with me ended up making first time confessions of faith and a lot more returned to their first love (Jesus). I'm convinced that these conversions happened *despite* my hapless attempts to instruct people and *because* Jesus loves others much more than I'm able to demonstrate.

However, since I've begun 'showing *and* telling,' instead of simply 'telling,' others about Jesus, I've witnessed a multiplication of souls coming to Christ.

Before anyone accuses me of putting forth the idea that 'my way is better than your way' allow me to clarify:

If God has put it on your heart to pursue the study of prophecy, tithing, spiritual gifts or anything else, PLEASE follow His lead. It may be that He WANTS you to concentrate solely on one particular facet of His Word for a particular reason or season. If that's the case, then I'd tell you to 'go for it with your whole heart.'

I simply believe that, since we are supposed to be like Jesus in how we deal with others, it's a great idea to follow the examples we're shown in the Scriptures of how He managed to touch the lives of so many. Jesus was a master teacher. Almost no one I've ever met (though there have been a couple) would debate this point. As such, when we look at how He taught people we can see that His overarching teachings were focused on '*the spiritual well-being of others.*'

A person who concentrates on the recording of the many miracles Jesus and His followers performed that had to do with physical health might misunderstand the point of physical healing(s). Every single physical healing we're shown throughout the entirety of the Bible (<u>every</u> miracle for that matter) had a spiritual component to it that is, most often, readily apparent to the reader (even though it may not have been to the person(s) receiving or seeing the miracle at the time).

In my estimation, each and every miracle recorded in the Bible shows us an aspect of God's love for us – from the miracles that showed His sovereignty over nature (the parting of waters, turning water into wine, resurrections etc.) to those showing His extreme love for us as His creation (the blind being made to see, the lame being made to walk, the restoration of an ear that had been amputated by the Apostle Peter) – all of them.

As such, I'd caution you that while focusing on a single aspect of God's Word may be what God has called you to do He's NEVER released any of His children from doing what He's done from time immemorial – focusing on loving others.

In other words, even if you've been called to proclaim news about the prophetic found in the Bible and how it impacts and has impacted history, you are still called to be a well-rounded follower of Christ – someone who is able to discern the need(s) of the person(s) with whom God has connected you. For me, this has meant learning to be aware that the person to whom I want to witness about God's… *commands, mercy, prophetic news, kindness, sacrifice*... might, first, need to be shown grace-filled love before they can receive the greater revelation God has for them. This love might manifest itself in their needing to be fed, given a hug, taken to a movie or any number of other ways.

Put another way, often before a person is able to receive whatever spiritual truth I've got for him, he needs to shown that I care about him. I think that's the point of 2 Timothy 2:22-26 (NIV) which reads:

"Flee the evil desires of youth, and pursue righteousness, faith, love and peace, along with those who call on the Lord out of a pure heart. Don't have anything to do with foolish and stupid arguments, because you know they produce quarrels. And the Lord's servant must not quarrel; instead, he must be kind to everyone, able to teach, not resentful. Those who oppose him he must gently instruct, in the hope that God will grant them repentance leading them to a knowledge of the truth, and that they will come to their senses and escape from the trap of the devil, who has taken them captive to do his will."

If you remember that, to your Father (God), the person you're seeking to be a witness to is more important than anything else, then you'll be able to live Jesus out loud much more effectively. Saint Augustine may have had this principle in mind when he wrote: *"Trust the past to God's mercy, the present to God's love and the future to God's providence."*

Recently I talked to Betty, a Christian teacher, who is employed at a local Christian school and I learned about an attitude shown by some Christian parents and Christian children that is definitely not Christ-like.

Chapter 8

Showing Love to Those Who Aren't Normal

Betty has taught in both Christian and secular schools for over 30 years. The majority of these years she's spent with children who have special needs (from those who are mentally or physically challenged to those with behavioral problems). I don't remember how we got on the subject but the issue of Autism came up.

Betty told me that the most challenging and yet rewarding experiences she's had has been with children who struggled with Autism and it's near twin, Asperger's. She says the rewards of her work far outweighed the challenges she'd faced professionally. Betty talked about how every child she'd encountered with any form of Autism had a special 'gift.' Some were extremely gifted artists or mathematicians, others could sing beautifully and other children were simply brilliant – having a talent of being able to recite long passages of information without making a mistake.

Betty said she believed these were the children of dreams. Their minds were a bit on the outside of the spectrum of normal which made them exceptional in ways few people take time to actually see or understand. But, she lamented, due to the lack of understanding about Autism, most people who spent time around these children often saw them as nightmares.

This wonderful lady recounted for me a half dozen of the children she'd recently worked with – some who were severely autistic and others who were on the higher functioning edges of Asperger's. Without exception, she told me, each of these children are miracles – handiworks of God who have the potential for greatness. In her opinion, these children, even with their behavioral problems, are special – not because of their disability but, rather, because of the ability God's given them to see the world as those of us who are *normal* don't. Unfortunately, they are often excluded from 'normal' activities of life because of the frequent (or even infrequent) outbursts that causes others to become nervous or, in her own words, 'freaks people out.'

Betty said she understood how the 'abnormal' behavior of these children can be disconcerting to those who encounter it the first several times. But, she insists, unlike those who have outwardly visible physical disabilities (a severe limp, deformed facial features, a malformed limb, etc.) society, as a whole, is much less likely to attempt to understand the reason behind the outburst(s) but, rather, simply attribute it to 'bad behavior.' This lack of understanding makes it a struggle for those who have Autism or Asperger's to find a welcome fit into traditional community.

Regrettably, those who struggle with Autism or Asperger's are often ostracized by their peers because parents have advised their own children to 'stay away from Suzi or Peter' because of the 'way they act.' These same parents would chastise their children if they ever made fun of or avoided someone who had a physical challenge and would advise their children that 'just because Suzi doesn't have an arm doesn't mean that they can't be your friend.' But, when it comes to behaviors that aren't readily recognizable as being due to a disability (or different ability) they become hypocrites.

It was at this point I knew Betty wasn't talking solely about pre-Christians but those of us who have been purchased by the blood of Jesus Christ and cleansed by the same even though we were completely disabled by sin. Christians, who are supposed to live out their faith in Him by showing His love to others often refuse to do so to those who are different than we are. Whereas Christians proclaim Jesus as their Lord and the potential Savior to men and women – even those who are murders, prostitutes, drug users and worse – they sometimes turn away from children and adults simply because they're uncomfortable with their actions.

Part of Our Family's Story

As this teacher, whose experience spans nearly two-thirds of my own life, talked to me I became enraptured because her tale was hitting so close to home.

My son, whom I love dearly, has Asperger's. As such, he 'misbehaves' due to the fact that, emotionally, he's approximately two-thirds of his chronological age. He's thirteen but he often acts as though he were only eight or nine years old. This means that at the age of fifteen, he'll only be ten years old emotionally.

To make matters more complicated, my son, along with most children I've met who have Asperger's, is incredibly smart and articulate. Rather than making it easier to manage, these abilities actually mask the struggles he faces with Asperger's – especially to those who have no experience with the disorder.

My son was twelve before we received the official diagnosis of Asperger's but, even before then, his mother and I knew he was different. Fortunately, our son doesn't react to news of this type in a hyper-negative way so, when we told him what Asperger's was, he didn't get depressed but, simply processed the information as fact. He thought that once people knew about the reasons he has outbursts and can't emotionally handle things as well as kids his own age, people would understand. He thought all he needed to do was explain to those he was

71

friends with about Asperger's and everything would be okay. Honestly, my wife and I thought the same as far as it concerned our friends.

Unfortunately, we were all wrong.

Our son has found himself, at times, miserably alone because people don't want their children to associate with him. This confuses him because, at this point in his life, he simply is not capable of reacting to situations in ways his peers do. Believe me, we know. We live with him 24 hours a day and we see his heart and know how much he wants to be normal. But, as I often tell him, *'normal is sometimes overrated.'*

We've found, as Betty did, that when people first find out our son suffers from a genetic abnormality, they show a semblance of compassion. However, as soon as the Asperger's manifests in a manner that's socially unacceptable, people begin either looking at us as if our parenting skills are deficient or at our son as if he is too impaired (or ill-behaved) to associate with their children.

Not long ago a friend of my wife remarked, *"You can't blame Asperger's for the way your son acted in co-op last week. He's thirteen years old and he needs to learn how to behave appropriately."*

Dawn, who is extremely grace-filled, responded to her friend by pointing out that, *"Yes, Asperger's was the cause of our son's meltdown."* She admitted the socially unacceptable behavior exhibited by our son wouldn't have been unexpected from her friend's own eight-year-old daughter but, because of our son's height and build (he's five feet, six inches tall and weighs approximately 150 pounds), people expect him to be more mature than he can be.

Dawn made mention of a mutual friend who had suffered a traumatic brain injury at nearly 60 years old. She noted that he can no longer function at the emotional, physical or mental level of a healthy person his own age. She also called attention to the fact that while his impairment was visible (because of the paralysis accompanying the brain injury), our son looked, on the outside, as normal as any other pre-teen.

My wife culminated her defense by stating that, since the gentleman who had suffered from a brain-bleed wouldn't be expected to function at a higher level than he currently does because of a physical impairment, it was unfair to expect our son to function at a level he's physically incapable of. Her friend, after realizing she'd made a rash, blanket statement about our son's behavior – because Asperger's isn't outwardly discernible – apologized.

Thankfully, not everyone who associates with our son and our family feels the same. For instance, two of our very close friends (Gary and Melicia), who know of our son's struggle, have consistently attempted to get their son together with our son. The other two people we've found who can be depended upon to show both us and our son compassion is my wife's Uncle Fred and Aunt Margaret.

There are only two reasons I can think these people would be able to do this:

1) The Holy Spirit has taught them mercy and grace that supersedes any earthly concerns they may have because he's helped them understand that all of us have 'problems' that don't always manifest in physically, mentally or socially acceptable ways.

2) They care enough about our family to have taken the time to discern that, even though our boy sometimes causes a scene by acting out, complaining and crying, he's not a 'bad' child. They know that we try to teach him temperance, that he's got a gentle, caring spirit, that he trusts people to a fault and that he's *more* than people see on the outside. For this, I can't thank them enough.

If you know someone who struggles with Autism, Asperger's or any of the myriad of mental challenges people face please remember… these disorders aren't something the person can easily control. In fact, for those with extreme mental challenges, the behaviors accompanying the disorder will never (aside from a miracle of God) be able to be controlled. It's a lifelong challenge for the person afflicted by certain disorders to learn how to control their behaviors and to replace those that are not acceptable with those that are.

My discussion with Betty has obviously left an impression on me but it's not simply because my son has Asperger's. Instead, it's because I've been afflicted with physical disorders my entire life and, more recently, I've had to learn to manage a major mental disorder.

From the time I was born it seems as though my body has been in rebellion – almost like it wants to succumb to the ravages of life. I was born with two holes in my heart (a VSD and ASD), a necrotic (dead) spleen that was removed soon after I was born and a diaphragmatic hernia (an abnormal opening in the diaphragm that caused part of my stomach, liver and intestines to move into my chest cavity near my lungs) which caused me great respiratory distress. As such, I've lived with an impaired immune system my entire life and this has meant that I've been more susceptible to disease than most people. For instance, I've contracted many childhood illnesses such as Chicken pox, Respiratory Syncytial Virus (RSV), Coxsackievirus A16 (HFM), Influenza, Impetigo, Croup, as well as life-threatening pneumonias, Meningitis, Endocarditis and others. Further, due to a latent Epstein-Barr virus that had lain dormant in my body for over four decades, I recently developed Stage IV cancer of the head and neck which threatened to kill me in 2007. Fortunately, I didn't succumb to the cancer but, in mid-February 2008, I did die due to respiratory and cardiac arrest and a lack of oxygen to my brain. This has left me severely impaired.

Fortunately, my son and I, with the support of my wife (his mother) and our friends, are blessed enough to be able to live a relatively normal life. Just as fortunately, I'm able to empathize with those who suffer from mental or physical disorders.

I've shared these details with you not so you'll feel sorry for me or others who have to live with various disorders but, rather, because I know it's very hard to put yourself in the shoes of other people – especially those we don't know well. Still, I believe, with every fiber of my being, that this is what the Lord Jesus Christ commands and shows us how to do as long as we're willing. Not doing so (not trying to feel what others feel and acting in a supportive manner) is simply, in my estimation, a sin against the Living God as well as the person we meet.

This isn't to say that we should simply and blindly accept disabilities for what the world sees them as – an excuse. Rather, we should work towards understanding what the person, as well as those who are their caregivers, is going through and to see how we, as His hands and feet here on earth, can undergird them. This, in my opinion, is the Christ-like manner we're all called to demonstrate.

Jesus Loves the Abnormal

Betty's story really impacted me because of the ministry God has given us – namely 99 for 1 Ministries. The motto of our ministry is to serve the under-loved in our city and beyond. Often those we serve are considered the outcasts of society – people who are homeless, drug addicts, alcoholics, teens and adults and in-betweeners, prostitutes, drug dealers etc. – in other words, those who are abnormal.

Still, these are the people God has given us a heart for and who are the mainstay of our ministry. Frankly, most of those we minister to are misfits in one way or another. Some reek from needing a bath or from booze and they usually have very little money. Most of them have social skills akin to either a sedated snail or an abused, meth-crazed ferret with an attitude. But, they are all loved by God and as Christians we're *going* to be there for them.

Imagine how different the church you attend would be if everyone who attended had to be 'normal?' Who would decide what normal is? What about your preacher or pastor? If they were to get extremely excited about a message they believed had been given to them by God, would you think it was strange that they were 'strange' for actually believing God had communicated with them? Or what about those who have been healed by God from a horrible disease and who want to shout from the rooftops that God is REAL and that He MUST be accepted before you can go to Heaven and have life eternally? Would you be embarrassed for them or shouting with them?

If our attitude towards people with physical challenges is that we should work to help them thrive… how then should we treat those who are mentally, emotionally or spiritually challenged? Hopefully, we'll take charge of our feelings, begin to learn why they behave the way they do and then teach our children that 'just because Suzi or Peter is different' doesn't mean they can't be your friend.'

Question: When you read the Bible, how often do you read of God using, in a mighty way, *normal* people?

Of course, you can find those who are 'normal' in the Bible being used by God but, more often than not, it's those we'd call abnormal whom God chooses to do His bidding. (Ex: God has used drunks and murderers, those who are stubborn and manic, zealots, beautiful people as well as plain, people who were willing to walk around naked and who, I'm certain would be committed to asylums by the standards we have today, people who are on the fringes of society and, when the occasion called for it, He even used animals.) Today, He has even chosen to use me – a short, middle-aged, bald guy who claims he's died, went to Heaven and came back to tell His story to all who will listen.

Christ, through His redeeming love for us, has eternally redefined the concept of normal. Not a single Christian should ever claim to be normal for the simple reason that we worship THE God of all and have been made anew by Him – a personal God, a living God and a God who defies and defied mortal rationality by giving up His throne, becoming like those He created, sacrificing His own life for those who killed Him and by loving those who hate Him.

Normal? No.

Awesome? Absolutely!

If you struggle with an affliction (mental, physical, emotional or spiritual), please know that GOD LOVES YOU and He wants His children to

LOVE YOU TOO!

Remember: Even though our perception of what God has done may seem like He has created a flawed person… God does NOT make mistakes! Regardless of how much we dislike the behavior or disability (even if we are the person afflicted) we, as His children, are called to love those who are hurting.

A second story I'd like to relate to you occurred around Thanksgiving. To me, what you're about to read illustrates the truth that if we follow God rather than worrying about what the world thinks then our lives will be happier.

The young lady and her family I tell about in the following story were used to teach me humility, sacrifice and that love really does trump all the other gifts the Holy Spirit might be willing to bestow upon us. More than this, God used their lives to show me what it means to be dependent upon God.

Chapter 9

A Dance With Eternal Impact

Very recently I was asked to bring some clothes for a little girl (7 years old) whose family was having a difficult time – one of the families we're trying to gather Christmas money for. I had no information other than that her name was Lindsey, her dress size was a 7 and that she wanted either sleeveless or short sleeves dresses and/or shirts. I was also told she liked clothes that 'poofed-out' when she spun around. I was assured that even if I couldn't find short-sleeved shirts her mom could hem them.

Armed with only that information I went to our storage shed (which is bursting with clothes for children thanks to the donations from people who have given generously to 99 for 1 Ministries). Admittedly, I struggled to find clothes for a little girl with whom I'd never had contact (I didn't know her favorite color or how tall she was or the 'type' of material she'd really like – factors which I'm highly aware are very important to girls because I have an 8 year old daughter myself). In any case, in about two hours, I was able to find about a half dozen dresses, about the same amount of pants and a nice, warm coat.

It took me over an hour and a half to find Lindsey's home (a trailer that's kind of out in the boonies). When I drove up I was immediately greeted by 3 dogs (big dogs – the kind we have at our house), all of which were barking and growling and wagging their tails at the same time. Not being exceptionally brave – especially when it comes to animals that can take chunks out of me – I decided to call the family phone from the safety of my truck.

As luck would have it, their phone was busy. I tried redialing and even honking my horn a couple of times (which stirred the dogs up into a slobbering frenzy) but no one came to the door. After about 10 minutes I was annoyed. Annoyed to the point I thought about just leaving and having the family meet me somewhere that was more territorially friendly (such as anywhere their three dogs wouldn't be able to size me up as a snack food).

Just as I was about to put my truck into reverse I saw movement from inside the trailer. The curtains parted a bit and I saw a little girls face beaming from within. She quickly disappeared. Then, a few seconds later, her little face popped back into view and I could tell she was calling out to someone inside the trailer.

Soon enough a woman came to the door, called her dogs inside and yelled for me to wait just a few minutes while she put them in their crates. I was more than happy to do so.

A couple of minutes later the mother walked out of her front door, came to my truck and invited me inside. I grabbed the plastic bags I'd brought Lindsey's clothes in and, as I walked towards the door of their home, I heard Lindsey excitedly ask, "*Dad, is that the white pastor who is bringing me the dresses?*"

Though I didn't hear her father's response I knew he'd affirmed that he thought I was because I heard the squeal of delight that only a little girl

80

can make (the kind that's so shrill it can only be matched in decibels by the wail of a siren).

As soon as I walked into the door I was greeted by a man in a wheelchair whose hair was still dripping wet. It turned out his wife had been in the bathroom helping him get out of the bathtub when I first arrived which hindered them from coming out to meet me – and it also explained the short ramp his wife and I had just walked up. Darlene and George are huggers, just like me, so I immediately felt at ease. But, Lindsey wasn't anywhere around.

After explaining to me that Lindsey was extremely shy around strangers Darlene went to collect her daughter. George and I talked while I laid the clothes I'd brought his daughter on their couch. Several minutes later Darlene appeared with Lindsey peeking out from behind her as they walked towards me.

"Hi," I said. "*I didn't know what kind of dresses you liked so I picked the ones I thought my own daughter would like.*"

When Lindsey finally spied all of the clothes that were behind me (I'd knelt down to her level) her eyes came to life and, without warning, she ran to me to give me a hug.

Folks, I've got to tell you, I can't remember ever feeling as awkward as I did in that moment.

Lindsey ran to me so quickly that I wrapped my arms around her before I realized that she had no arms. Instead, she laid her face against my neck and kind of snuggled with me. The hug was over in a moment and she asked Darlene, "*Mommy, can I try this one on?*"

Lindsey had chosen the brightest, most multi-colored dress in the bunch (my daughter calls them gypsy dresses because of a play she was in once). George told Lindsey she could try them on after I left because he was certain I had a lot of other business to take care of. As just about any seven year old who is excited would do, Lindsey pleaded and, after I said

I could spare a few minutes, her parents capitulated and the little girl picked the dress up in her lips and ran towards her bedroom – her mother following behind.

After being sincerely thanked by George and offered a cold drink, he and I began to talk. To make a long story short, here's a synopsis of what I found out while Lindsey was changing into her new clothes:

Darlene and he had been married for nearly 12 years before Lindsey had come along. Due to some type of birth defect, Lindsey had been born without her left arm and only a partial right arm (which, eventually, had to be amputated because the bone in it was severely deformed and was causing their daughter agonizing pain). George had lost the total use of his right leg and only had partial use of his left leg after being involved in a car wreck.

Darlene is a stay-at-home mom who homeschools Lindsey (who should be in the 2nd grade but who is doing 4th grade work – that should sound familiar to any homeschooling parent) and George is on partial disability because he still teaches welding part-time and Lindsey loves to dance. They've been having a difficult time due to the fact that George can't teach full-time and they're still paying off medical bills related to Lindsey's rehab. Due to the cost of rehab, they'd lost the house they had lived in for nearly 10 years and they currently live in the trailer because of the kindness of Darlene's brother (whom I have since met and who is a terrific guy). To say that George was thankful I'd driven all the way from Mobile to deliver clothes to a little girl I'd never met would be an understatement.

After several minutes, Lindsey bounced back into the living room and she was absolutely beaming! Excitedly she asked if I wanted to see a 'new dance' she'd recently made up to one of her favorite songs. Of course I said "*Yes.*"

Immediately she went to their stereo system, used her forehead to pop-open the glass doors and then took a pen in her mouth and began manipulating the controls on the stereo with amazing precision. Soon enough she'd found the track she wanted, pressed play and ran out into the middle of the living room. For several minutes Lindsey danced and pranced around the room, whirling and twirling so that the 'gypsy dress' flared out in different directions and made plumes of color around her caramel-colored legs. By the time Big Daddy Weave's *Audience of One* was done I was in tears but was smiling from ear to ear. I stayed at the trailer long enough for Lindsey to model each one of the dresses I'd brought for her.

After a few more hugs and being introduced to each one of their dogs I was escorted to my truck by the three of them, given one final snuggle by Lindsey and I was off to see someone in a local hospital.

As I drove away from their home I became completely overwhelmed by emotion and had to pull my truck over. I sat, alone in a parking lot, weeping. I wept not only because God had allowed me to make contact with such a precious family but also because my children are, by and large, whole.

I thought of the way Lindsey had danced with such joy and I realized that, after a few minutes of seeing her dancing, in my mind I was 'seeing' my own daughters hands and arms making motions in the air – fluid strokes of pure passion that I see her do almost every single day when she dances for my wife and I. Then I began crying more because I realized Lindsey doesn't recognize herself as 'handicapped' and, because of that, she really isn't.

I think it's rare for us to really know what we're thankful for. But, as for me, I know what I'm thankful for and it's more than the fact that God has given me healthy children. Rather, I'm thankful He has allowed me to become infected with His love for others and that He allows all of us who are willing to share His love with others and to meet people who will be eternally impacted by this love. We, in turn, are positively changed by the same.

My question to you is this: What are you thankful to God for?

As a follow-up to this story, George, Darlene and Lindsey have since moved out of state and George is now a full-time foreman for a steel factory (thanks to a reader of our newsletter who asked to be put in contact with the family). Darlene is still a stay-at-home, homeschooling mom and Lindsey is happily performing at a dance studio in their local area.

Chapter 10

Treat Everyone As If They Are a *Pre*-Christian Rather Than a *Non*-Christian

I've thought long and hard about the words we use. While I don't think that the universe is governed by our words nor do I believe we can speak things into existence by the power of the words that come from our mouths, I certainly believe they're powerful in that they're the way we communicate. Most everyone, with the notable exceptions of existential nihilists, atheists, some forms of Buddhism, the followers of Jean Paul Sartre and a few others, agree that the meaning we apply to words have a direct impact on how we perceive the world around us.

Any doubt as to the impact of words will be dispelled if you follow political commercials or advertisements that tout the benefits of one product over another. Certain experts argue that a single word can win or lose a customer. So serious is this theory that entire courses on choosing a word or a group of words are offered on campuses and seminars the world over.

While I might deny certain theological and secular tenants as they relate to words, I do agree we should be careful as to the labels we use. For instance, which do you think would get more votes on a ballet... one that was called 'Pro-Death' or 'Pro-Choice?' The question is, of course, rhetorical.

While the above comparison might ruffle some feathers I used it to make a point. For most Christians it's common to think of a person who hasn't yet committed their lives to Christ as Non-Christian. While this definition is certainly accurate I don't think it's as beneficial as thinking of the same group as being pre-Christians. The difference should be obvious – the term non-Christian carries with it the baggage of decades of anti-Christian sentiment whereas the term pre-Christian holds an unstated hope that those we encounter may, at some point, become a family member in Christ. Which group would you rather spend your time ministering to and which would you be more likely to devote more time to – a non-Christian or a pre-Christian?

The nature of the last two questions will hopefully draw your attention to the fact that we tend to 'judge books by their covers' more often than we should. Sometimes we do this literally (for instance, you may have chosen to begin reading this book, *Living Jesus Out Loud,* because of the artwork or title) but, for the most part, I'm talking about the way we judge *people* based on our perceptions of who we *think they are* rather than who we *believe they can become*.

It's been my experience that perception has a tendency to be reality for most people – including Christians. The reason this is terribly disturbing and potentially deadly (spiritually speaking) is because perceptions are almost never correct. Allow me to give you two true 'for instances' of how perceptions can be horribly skewed even when we have the best intentions and would never, in our wildest dreams, believe we'd think ill or good of a person without good reason.

Case #1 – Frank

Frank goes to my church. He's a nice fellow. He made a public profession of faith in Jesus Christ nearly 2 years ago and was baptized. Since then, Frank has attended practically every church function we've held, he serves on two teams (greeters and ushers), he faithfully gives his tithe (10% of the gross amount of money he and his wife make), gifts (money and other donations above and beyond his tithe), actively promotes Christ's love, His grace, His mercy and he has a heart-wrenching story as to how Jesus changed his life.

Case #2 – Harold

Harold goes to my church. He doesn't smile much – frankly, most of the time, he wears a scowl. He's not extremely friendly and, to my knowledge, he's never been baptized (at least not publicly). No one knows much about Harold because he keeps to himself and rarely publicly prays for anyone. Plus, Harold occasionally smokes a cigar, he's been divorced and, from time to time, he's been known to have an occasional beer or margarita.

Based on the above descriptions of Frank and Harold, which one do you think most people would think (perceive) is a Christian? The man most people choose is Frank. However, as you've probably already guessed, there's more to these stories than you've been allowed to know. What I've given you is the *cover story* – the outside picture that most people see and make a judgment based upon. The inside story – the part of these men that few take the time to get to know – is where the real truth is.

Harold's Story

While it's true Harold isn't seen as friendly it's because he really does scowl quite a bit. Though he's been trying to change this, his 'scowl' is simply the way his face looks when he's either relaxed or intently concentrating. Frankly, when Harold is concentrating in prayer I think he looks as if he's downright angry. But, he's not. It's also true that Harold rarely prays for anyone and that he keeps to himself but this is because he's a very shy man. And, while he does occasionally smoke cigars he actually gave up a two-pack-a-day cigarette habit years ago and, while he does have an occasional drink (I've never seen him drunk or even tipsy), Harold also has a proverbial heart of gold.

Those who have known Harold for several years have independently verified the story he's told me of his conversion to Christ. It was while he was in Iran in the early 1980's. Harold wasn't anywhere near the frontlines of battle when he gave his life to Jesus. In fact, he was eating lunch with a couple of friends when, according to every account of the story, Harold unexpectedly broke down in tears. His friends, all of them 'rough and tough Marines,' didn't know what to do or say. Harold, not known as the most talkative person in their unit, began to speak through his tears and told the five sitting with him in the mess tent that his second wife had been diagnosed with cancer and, to make matters worse, she wanted a divorce from him because he'd been, by his own admission, an inattentive husband who, according to his wife, acted more like a drill sergeant than the loving man she'd married years ago.

To say that least, Harold was a broken man. His tour was still almost a year from being complete but the only thing he wanted was to be home with his wife. He admitted to his friends that he'd actually considered harming himself in order to get stateside so he could work on his marriage.

Tim, one of the guys Harold was eating with that day asked him, point blank, if he'd asked Jesus to intervene in their lives. Harold recalls his tears almost immediately abated and that he looked up at his friend with a look of absolute anger. Harold claims he thought to himself, '*How dare this guy suggest some 'pie-in-the-sky,' ridiculous suggestion to solve my real life crisis.*' But, Tim insisted on praying for both Harold and his wife and, instead of waiting for permission, he simply began speaking.

Harold told me, "*I thought the guy was a closet nut-job. I mean, I'd fought alongside Tim for nearly 2 years, sometimes in extremely hairy situations and I knew that he prayed every morning, at every meal and at bedtime and even during combat but I just thought it was a crutch he used to get through the times. But, when Tim prayed this time, his head was bowed, his brow was furrowed and he seemed intent on praying for my wife, Lori, and me. All the other men had followed his lead and had bowed their heads and closed their eyes. I just stared at Tim for almost a minute as he prayed something about how Lori's mind would be changed by God, that she and I would realize that Jesus could connect us again in a way that we'd never be able to imagine if we both accepted Him as our Lord and Savior and that either the cancer in Lori's body would be taken away or that we'd be given the strength to get through the disease and come out of the ordeal with our faith strengthened."*

According to Harold, by the time he decided to lower his head so that he wouldn't be the only one not doing so the soldier abruptly stopped praying. Tim stood up, put his hand on Harold's shoulder and said something the hurting man would never forget, *"Jesus knows you and loves you and Lori. But, it's up to you to get to know Him. Talk to me later if you'd like to find out how."*

With that they all finished their meals in silence and broke for the evening. Later that night, when Harold couldn't sleep because the man's words kept running through his mind, 'Jesus knows you and loves you and Lori,' he went to his friend's tent and found Tim reading through the Bible.

Harold says, *"I'll remember until my dying day the smile Tim had as I walked into his tent. He got up, shook my hand and said, 'So, you're either here to cuss me out or to learn about Jesus. So, which one is it?' I was so emotionally broken I could only get out one word… 'Jesus.' Tim told me, 'I was hoping you'd say that. Sit down and tell me what you know about Jesus."*

Harold says the conversation he had about his knowledge of Jesus was not only very short but, as it turned out, extremely wrong.

He states, *"Tim never let on that I was a moron. Instead, for the next six or so hours, he patiently guided me through the Bible, starting way back in the Old Testament, and showed me that Jesus was throughout the Bible. He also told me his own personal story and how he knew, for a fact, that Jesus was still in the miracle working business. At the end of our study it was time for us to go on duty. Tim prayed that neither he nor I would suffer fatigue because of the time we'd spent studying God's word and do you know what… neither of us did – at least I didn't. I pulled a 12-hour shift and was completely energized at the end of the day. Tim looked about as refreshed as I did. I'd had all day to think about what Tim had said the night before and I knew that I was ready to accept Jesus as my Lord and Savior – as my God.*

I found Tim and we went behind a Caterpillar tractor where he asked me to tell God what I was feeling, that I wanted him to be my God and that I knew and believed that His Son, Jesus, had lived, died for my sins and that He had been resurrected to show that He had power over life and death. I did exactly what Tim told me to do and I guess I was expecting some kind of light show to happen, but, afterwards, I didn't really feel any better. Tim told me that this was okay because I'd just been born again so I was literally less than a minute old spiritually speaking. He assured me that if I'd been serious about my belief in God that I was now adopted as God's son and that I now had direct access to ask my new Father for things that I knew would make Him happy. Boy, did I jump on that.

It was going to be another 7 hours before I'd be able to call my wife so I began talking to my new Father about all the things I wanted to change about me so that Lori wouldn't want to leave. I told him I really needed for Him to give Lori someone there at home so that she wouldn't be alone when she went through all her cancer treatments. Then I remembered Tim had prayed that the cancer that had invaded her body would just be gone so I must have talked to God about that for nearly five hours."

To make a long story much shorter, Harold called Lori that morning (her time) and they talked for over an hour about Harold's new relationship with Jesus. At first Lori was skeptical but she seemed to like Harold's new passion for her and for God. She told him she'd wait to file for a divorce until they had talked about it more.

The next week Lori called Harold and told him something that changed both of their lives: The doctors had confirmed that the tumors in her breasts had significantly reduced in size and, though they still planned to do a double mastectomy, they told her she had a few more weeks to determine when the best time would be for her to schedule the operation. She begged Harold to come home but he'd already confirmed that there was no way for him to do so. Instead, empowered by what had been done by who he thought must have been God, Harold suggested that Lori pray with him that the Holy Spirit would completely remove the cancer from her breasts. Reluctantly and very skeptically, she agreed and so Harold prayed for his wife. Due to the fact that Harold had gone on maneuvers and was unable to contact Lori during them, he called her three weeks later. Lori told her husband, with a very excited, tear-filled voice, that her oncologists had confirmed that the cancer she had was suddenly and inexplicably in total remission! No mastectomy, no treatments! Two weeks later Lori also gave her life to Christ and, today, at the time of this book, they've both been Christians for around three decades.

The long and short of this story is that Frank and Harold are BOTH Christians. Frank's commitment to Jesus is simply easier to 'spot' than Harold's. But what Harold lacks in personality he more than makes up by befriending soldiers who are returning to the States and who are still overseas and both he and Lori have begun an online (Skype-based) counseling program designed to help husbands and wives work on their marriages even if they're separated for years and by distances rarely experienced by their civilian counterparts.

Again, it just goes to show that we shouldn't judge a book by its cover but, rather, by its content. The following testimony illustrates what I mean when it comes to not judging others by the way they look on the outside.

Chapter 11

Buying Gas For the Sake of Jesus

Several years ago I learned the hard way to not judge a book by its cover by doing exactly that. It happened while we were doing a community outreach called a Gas Buy Down.

[Note: A gas buy down is a simple thing to do for practically any group or church – even if your budget is only a few hundred dollars. It's also what I would categorize as a 'soft touch' outreach in that Christians are able to connect with many people but only briefly. A soft touch outreach rarely turns into anything greater than a friendly '*Hey, how are you?*' type of association but it's a tremendous way to let lots of people know the body of Christ is alive, well and active.]

Once, just before a gas buy down, I was asked by a man why we'd chosen such an outreach. When I told him it was because we believed that Jesus would do the same if He were on earth today he asked, with a dubious tone, "*You think Jesus would buy gas for people?*"

I replied, "*Of course. Jesus met people where they were and ministered to them by giving them what they needed. Sometimes it was food, other times it was water, often it was a physical healing or prayer. So, why not gasoline?"*

My response seemed to satisfy the man and, since that day, I've participated in at least twenty gas buy downs and he's joined us in around five.

In trying to set-up another gas buy down I had contacted a couple of gas stations in our area and, after a week, had not gotten a response from any of them. On a whim (or the leading of the Holy Spirit), my wife, Dawn, decided to call the Murphy's station located just inside a heavily visited Wal-Mart Supercenter parking lot and asked if we could give away gas.

Her initial phone call was met with surprise but not a negative answer. Justin, the person on duty, had to call his manager (Cynthia) who, in turn had to contact the district manager for the Murphy gas stations in Daphne and Mobile Alabama. To make a long story short, after a couple of clarifying conversations (they wanted to make certain we weren't planning on badgering anyone who didn't happen to agree with our particular religious views), we got permission to do the event.

I found out later that getting permission from a district manager for our program was akin to witnessing a miracle. Due to the potential problems people have with others participating in any kind of religious activity in the public arena, it's simply easier and usually less likely to involve legal questions, to *'Just say No.'*

Frankly, I think this outreach was God-ordained. Maybe it wasn't, but I figure I'll give Him the credit until He tells me otherwise.

Anyway, it was great. One of our church members, David – a former army sergeant – joined Dawn and me as we gave away gas. The tag line we used to introduce what we were doing for those who pulled up to the pump was simple:

"We know you need gas, so we'd like to buy you $5 worth for free – no strings attached."

When asked why we were doing this, our response was just as simple:

"To show the love of Jesus in a practical way."

The response to this outreach was overwhelmingly positive.

When my wife told one lady we were going to buy her $5 of gas she threw open her car door, jumped out and gave Dawn a bear hug. This shocked me because by this time Dawn, David, and I were soaking wet with sweat (the heat index was already topping 100 degrees).

Another lady bought us bottled water just to say 'thanks for being so kind to everyone' and many people marveled that people would be taking time out of their day to buy something for people they didn't even know.

David was able to assist a gentleman whose car needed a jump – I don't think the engine ever started but just the fact David was there and offered to help him was a major blessing.

During the entire time we were at the station, only two people refused to let us buy them gas. One gentleman begged off by stating there were other people who could probably use it more than he could (a perfectly honorable response) while the other was just too suspicious. After we'd given him a $5 Wal-Mart gas card, he mulled our proposition over 'Free Gas – No Strings Attached' and finally gave it back saying, *"Nah, nothing's free. There's gotta be a catch."*

When I heard his response the first thing I thought is that this man has been hurt – probably often. He's one of those Christians need to be on the lookout for to show that some things really are free – such as love, etc.

Technically, people are correct when they say the things we do on outreaches aren't really free. They do cost someone something, just not them. We who do outreaches and those who support us are the ones paying the cost so the people we meet can receive something with zero strings attached.

If you're a Christian that concept should sound very familiar because it's what happens in our exchange with Jesus – He gives us His righteousness which He paid an infinite price for. But, we get to call it '*Free.*' Kind of neat, isn't it? Through outreach to our neighbors and to people we don't know and may never meet again, we get to taste a very small sample of what Jesus did for us – we give of ourselves, of what we have worked for, without any guarantee that what we're offering will be accepted.

Okay, here's a confession... I, like many others, sometimes judge a book by its cover. Fortunately, I don't often allow my initial judgment jade me one way or the other – good or bad – because I know my surface judgment needs to be balanced by a deeper inspection of the person or situation. But, I don't always succeed...

A young African American gentleman pulled up to the pumps driving a rather beat-up older red car – a car whose 21" rims and tires probably cost more than the rest of the vehicle in its entirety. The driver had very long dreadlocks and the stereo was blasting rap music.

My first thought was (and I'm being very honest), "*Sigh, I don't want to waste the gas card on this guy.*"

That was what my 'flesh' thought. Then, the Holy Spirit convicted me and my spirit immediately rejoiced and I thought, "*I'm so glad this man has come here today! This might be the last day he's not a Christian!*"

Even though my flesh was weak, my thoughts were taken captive by the spirit of Christ and I was able to approach this man, whose exterior presented someone rough and tough and potentially dangerous, with a heart of compassion and friendliness.

I said our tag line to him and his entire demeanor changed. Where he had not been smiling, he smiled. Where he and I at one time might not have ever exchanged pleasantries, we did.

I don't have to wonder what Jesus' response to me would have been had I not served this gentleman. He wouldn't have been pleased. As such, I wouldn't have been pleased with myself. Frankly, I don't know what this man's story is. Perhaps he was and is a Christian who simply chose to listen to music that I didn't listen to (I don't always listen to Christian music). And what about his car – so what if I don't have the same taste in vehicles (or maybe the car wasn't even his – he might have borrowed it)?

My point is: This man, just like you and me, are made in the image of Almighty God. He is loved by God, Jesus died for him and the Holy Spirit wants him to become His child (if he's not already). So, if I'm going to be a true ambassador for King Jesus, if I'm going to try to do His will on Earth, then I have to be willing not to jump to conclusions.

Actually, that's not true. *ALL Christians should immediately jump to a conclusion. The conclusion we should jump to is that every person we meet deserves our respect because they are made in the image of Our God and Father and He wants us to treat others the way He treats us – with love.*

As a local church growth method soft touch outreach efforts are rarely successful. But, as a method to grow the universal body of Christ it can be extremely effective. Soft touch outreaches such a gas buy down fall into the category of '*raising the spiritual water level of all churches.*' Soft touch outreaches are events such as water and newspaper giveaways, community efforts like cutting the grass in fields where children play or BBQ's in neighborhoods that are done for the sole reason of introducing people to one another, etc.

Unfortunately, because this type of outreach doesn't often directly impact the numbers of people who actually show-up at a specific church, they aren't very popular with most Christians. This is unfortunate because, as I'm about to illustrate, they are tremendous for building relationships within your own church as well as between congregations.

Chapter 12

A Few Gallons of Gas and
A Few Dozen Tears

One night, in late November, as I left my house I didn't feel all that well. In fact, I wanted nothing more than to stay in bed most of the day and, by the time I was on the road, all I felt like doing was crawling under the covers, closing my eyes and heading towards dreamland. God had other plans.

After going to two different hospitals (some forty miles away from each other) and having ministered to two different families I was finally heading back towards my house. My wife had called earlier in the evening and asked that I stop by Wal-Mart and I'd hesitantly agreed to do so. As all of you who live in the Mobile area know, night time in November can be very cold and windy – this night was both and I wasn't really looking forward to staying out any later than necessary. This state of mind almost cost me one of the best nights of ministry I've experienced.

Cruising down the highway towards my exit I noticed a white suburban-type truck near the shoulder. Honestly, I wouldn't have given it a second glance had I not also seen, just barely, something that looked like a piece of white rag, waving towards the roadway, just at the height of the rear window. Without much thought I simply changed lanes so I'd be in the middle lane away from the truck. As I zoomed past I saw that the 'white rag' was attached to the arm of a lady. It's amazing the amount of detail the human eye can perceive in a fraction of a second. I noted that the white I'd seen was actually the sleeve of a white blouse beneath a dark sweater or jacket that held within them a black lady whose dark brown hand was waving frantically towards any and every car coming her direction. By the time I'd taken all of this in I was several hundred yards away and her truck was becoming smaller and smaller in my rearview mirror.

In an instant I'd thought to myself, *'Someone will help her.'* AND *'Why doesn't she have a cell phone to call someone instead of standing on the side of the road trying to wave people down at night?'* AND *'It's cold outside and I need to get to Wal-Mart.'*

Honestly, those were almost my exact thoughts. Then, nearly immediately, I felt the Lord speak to my heart and I audibly, though slightly reluctantly, said, "*Okay God. You got me. I'll turn around and go see if she needs help.*"

Within a few minutes I'd driven about three miles back towards her on a service road. As I pulled beside her, blocked by a high, chain link fence, I blinked my lights on and off until she noticed me and stepped towards my car. After a few minutes I knew she'd ran out of gas, that she had no money for more gasoline and that her daughter, whom she'd been trying (but had failed) to contact via her cell phone, lived near Creola (almost forty miles away). A minute or so later she'd thrown me a single, one-gallon, plastic gas container over the fence and about ten minutes later (after having gone to a gas station) I pulled up behind her disabled vehicle.

Minutes before, as I had filled the container, I'd noted that the spout didn't work correctly but, I thought, we'd figure out how to get the fuel into her truck once I was there. Just after I drove up behind her and turned on my flashers the lady stepped into view holding several pieces of notebook paper. As I retrieved the gas container she opened the fuel door and begin folding the papers into a funnel and placing them into the gas tank. *"Obviously,"* I thought, *"This isn't the first time she's run out of gas."*

Once she'd cranked her truck I asked her to follow me to a nearby station so I could put fuel into her vehicle and, minutes later, I was standing outside of her truck, fueling it up and talking to her.

I handed her one of our 99 for 1 Ministries cards and introduced myself as Lonnie. She looked at the card and absently told me her name was Angie. She looked from the card to me to the card again and finally her eyes glued to my own. As Angie and I looked at one another, I saw tears streaming down her face. She asked, *"So, you're a Reverend?"*

I said yes and was about to say something else but was stopped because Angie, suddenly and quite unexpectedly, burst into full-blown sobbing. Her sobs weren't of joy but, rather, mournful. To say I was startled would be an understatement. Not knowing exactly what to do I simply continued to fill her truck.

A few seconds or minutes later (I can't tell you which because I was desperately praying God would give me some insight as to why she was crying), Angie composed herself enough to tell me the following.

"Pastor Honeycutt, I used to be saved but I've backslidden something awful the past few years. I meant to go to church this last Sunday but I didn't because when I got up all I had was a Winter dress and it was pretty warm so I thought I'd wait until it was colder to go. I knew I was wrong in waiting but I did anyway. You know, this morning I had to call the police on my husband of 21 years and have him taken to jail because he was doing drugs and hurting me." She paused, brushed a few new tears from her eyes, took a deep, ragged breath and continued. *"I was just in my truck praying God would allow me to come back into His life when I ran out of gas. I must have been there for at least forty-five minutes and I couldn't get hold of*

anyone on my cell phone and suddenly you pull up. I can't believe... actually I DO believe that God loves me so much that out of all the cars that passed me by tonight He'd wait until you, a pastor, would see me and stop and help me. Thank you!"

With that she leaned in, gave me a big smooch on my cheek and an even bigger hug. A few minutes later I left her with the suggestion that she give us a call if she or her husband (even while he was in jail) needed anything. She said she would and left.

Folks, I didn't know if I would ever see Angie again in this life. But, I promise you we were both impacted that night and both of us have God to thank. Thinking back on what happened, I'm amazed – not only at the number of cars that must have gone past Angie but also because I almost became one of them (a person who sees someone on the side of the road, thinks to himself that 'someone' will surely stop to help them and then forgetting the person by the time your vehicle has passed over the next hill).

Instead, I was blessed because I met a lady who'd just spoken to God, seeking an affirmation of His love towards her, and I was used by God to show the same.

I didn't hear anything from Angie for over six months after I'd filled her tank with fuel and, frankly, when I did 'hear' from her I'd completely forgotten who she was until she reminded me and I found the above story in an email I'd sent (that's the problem with short-term memory loss – everything sort of slips away after a bit).

But, Angie did call me. Her husband, Devon, whom I've never met but with whom I'd apparently spoken at some time during the past six months, was released from jail about three months after Angie and I had met. He had taken the suggestion I'd made and contacted an in-house jail chaplain, given his life to Jesus and was, according to Angie, a changed man by the time he came home.

During the past four months she and her husband have begun attending a local church, both have gotten baptized and their four children

(Travius, Shatiqua, Angelina and Ben) have all gotten involved in community outreach and have invited several other churches in their area to join them.

Devon, who was at one time (by his own admission) a very abusive husband and father is voluntarily undergoing anger management courses through a Christian organization and, according to his wife and their pastor (who has invited me to speak to his flock about servant evangelism), is a completely changed man.

I tell you this story not to 'toot my own horn' (remember I almost drove away from Angie just like all the other people had done for nearly an hour) but, instead, so that we'll all remember to THANK GOD, the Living King of Kings, that He cares enough about everyone to connect two strangers so His love can be demonstrated.

What all of this means is that through one '*Act of Kindness with a Purpose*,' a seed was planted that eventually changed an entire family and has begun growing so that the Kingdom of God is advancing. Praise God!

The reason I love stories like the one I just related to you is because I played a relatively minor role in the big scheme of the story God had planned for this family. It goes to show that God can and does use us, for His glory and for the salvation of others (both eternally and temporally), if we're willing to be vessels of His love for others.

The night Angie and I met I began praying she and her family would be led by God to a church home (one filled with His children who would show them God's love and compassion). Of course, I invited them to visit the church I attended but I truly wanted God to help them choose where they'd begin attending. For all I knew our church wouldn't be the one for them (it wasn't). In fact, it could have been your church Angie and her family were drawn to. Either way, God's will and purpose in their lives would be accomplished. What more could we ask for?

Chapter 13

How the Seed of Servant Evangelism Was Planted In Me

Not unlike most people who undergo a radical transformation, the end-result of the change is often not seen for quite some time. The same could definitely be said about me and my journey towards being a sold-out believer in evangelizing people through service (living out the gospel of Jesus Christ rather than simply telling people about Him).

Not long ago (just over 4 years at the time of this writing) I was afflicted with Stage IV cancer of the head and neck (specifically oropharyngeal cancer). As a result of the diagnosis I underwent radical surgery which resulted in the removal of nine malignant tumors in my neck, head and chest, the removal of the base of my tongue as well as the extraction of a major nerve, six inches of muscle tissue (that left me with a reduced left trapezius) and my left jugular vein – all of which was followed by both radiation and chemotherapy treatments.

For those who are interested in reading about the treatment, how I handled the same and what happened after I died and before I rose again you should get a copy of my book *Death, Heaven and Back – The True Story of One Man's Death and Resurrection.*

For now, I would ask that you, the reader, simply take it for granted that this time in my life wasn't the best of times – in fact, it was during this period in our marriage that my wife lived up to her promise to love me regardless of whether we were rich or poor, in good health or bad and I am very happy to declare my love for the woman God gave to me.

I gave you a brief run-down as to what my family and I were going through because it helps put in perspective why I wrote the following letter (which is found starting on page 173 in the aforementioned book). It's in response to a corporation that had chosen to 'adopt' my family during Christmas. It's my personal testimony of how God sometimes (I think more often than we're aware) works in the lives of those who are years from becoming His children to direct their later attitudes. The story you're about to read confirms, at least to me, one of the reasons I eventually became convinced that servant evangelism is the way to reach people.

Christmas for the Honeycutts

With Christmastime approaching, my wife and I were having a frank talk about what Christmas Day would look like. Perhaps it was because I was on pain-killers that I'd never considered the impact that co-pays, medical stays and other cancer-related issues would take on our finances until that night. In any case, I was totally unprepared when my wife looked me squarely in my eyes and made the matter-of-fact statement: *"Lonnie, we have NOTHING for Christmas."*

While I tried to minimize the impact that her statement had on me, I didn't sleep for nearly two days. I kept running scenarios through my mind that might allow me to create a flow of income that would not only benefit my family but also some of the people we know who are in dire straits.

The realization that my body was simply not able to function like it had been able to two months ago – meaning that my strength (both physical and mental) and my emotions were on uncontrollable, virtual roller coaster rides, was like a slap in the face. It became apparent I would need to talk with my children about Christmas this year.

Please don't get me wrong. In my family we really do value what Christmas means even without gifts but, for a four and an eight-year-old, the understanding that presents aren't going to be a part of the season is just a bit harder to grasp. To say the least, I was dreading this conversation.

With that being said, I'd like to say that your ability, both personally and as a corporate whole, to grasp some sense of the desperation my wife and I felt in having to deal with the ordeal of cancer, the treatment of the same and the expense involved, especially as the Christmas season approached, is commendable.

Allow an ailing man to tell you a brief story...

At the tender age of 8 years old (the same age I find my own son today), around the time of Christmas, my family and I were living in the foothills of the Carolinas in a one-room shack (it was literally a shack designed to serve as a repose for hunters rather than as a house for a family).

To say we were poor would be an understatement of grand proportions. The floor on which we walked was made of warped 2" x 4"s so unevenly spaced you could see dirt below them. My mother, in an attempt to reduce cold drafts as much as possible, stuffed newspaper in-between the boards. A single wood stove stood alone in the center of the one-room shack and served as both heater and cooking stove. When it came time for baths, my sister and brother (two and four years younger than me) and I would build a small fire in the backyard, fill a #3 washtub with a couple of inches of water (as much as the three of us could manage to carry without spilling it), warm the water and then carry it inside to a small porcelain tub. This procedure would be repeated four or five times until there was enough water to soak all of us.

As the eldest child and, as the resident pyromaniac, it was my job to chop wood, prepare fires and make coffee for my mother. I can't help but imagine that to most children the preparation of a cup of coffee would rank somewhere around tooth extraction and fingernail clipping on a 'fun scale.' As I grew older I came to realize the reason I relished making coffee for my mom was because in doing so I could show her a modicum of love. You see, we didn't own a coffee pot. Instead, I would fill a small tin cup with water, scoop a small amount of instant coffee into it, stir it slightly and patiently hold it over the flickering flame of a single candle, my fingers wrapped in a washcloth so as to not be burned, until the dark, bitter liquid bubbled. I'm quite certain that Mom never even got an adequately tasty cup of coffee from my hands but she never let on. To this day, making those cups of coffee ranks high on my favorite list of memories.

It's rare for me to share what I've just shared concerning my early childhood days because the memories are sometimes painful and difficult to relate. The reason I've chosen to do so is because I sincerely believe that the events that took place during this period of time helped to mold me into the man I am today. It's important for us to remember that the seemingly small, almost insignificant actions we take can have a major impact on others. Read on...

Though our home didn't have a television or, from what I can remember, even a radio, it was evident that Christmas was right around the corner. The children of our neighbors, who were ostensibly just as poor as we were, had done what kids do – they made ready for the special day of presents with what they had at hand. Colorful bottle caps from soft drinks and beer were pierced with a nail (there were no pop-tops or plastic tops then) and strung together with yarn, brightly designed paper snowflakes of assorted sizes were taped to windows and on windowsills there were propped, looking outward, a hodge-podge of Christmas elves, Santas, evergreen trees and reindeer – most of which looked either horribly skinny or bloated from too many Christmas cookies. The memory of these trinkets, along with the expectant excitement of the children who lived on our side of town, has seared into my heart an almost palpable sense of what Christmas feels like – in two words: hope and wonder.

Though I didn't realize it fully at the time, the reality of what Christmas morning was really going to look like for my family was bearing down on my parents. My father, a full-time, long-haul trucker had been out of work, except for the occasional monthly run between two states, for nearly three months. Plus, whatever extra money my dad seemed to be able to get was spent on alcohol (he was a major and brutally mean drunk). My mother, having three young children to care for and no transportation had done what she could to earn money so that she could keep us fed, however leanly, for weeks. Still, while we had shelter over our heads, drafty but warmish beds in which to sleep and two parents who loved us dearly, dad and mom knew that this would provide very little solace the morning after Santa was supposed to have arrived.

Unbeknownst to anyone (even my parents) a small group of people had other plans for our home and several of those in our neighborhood. Late on Christmas Eve (it must have been nearing 5 p.m. because the sun was going down and most of the stores in town were closed or closing), three grown-ups appeared at our door. Mom knew two of them as members of a local church from where we occasionally collected food stamps and they were invited in. As I remember it, within minutes, my sister, Lillian, my brother, David, and I were all bundled up tightly and herded into a waiting station wagon. Even though I know it took much longer to arrive at the five and dime store (having driven to it as an adult), we seemed to only be in the backseat of the car for mere seconds. As youngsters, the time simply flew by.

Prior to departing, the grown-ups had quickly gathered notes on our sizes of shoes, pants, underwear, coats and other essentials from our parents. Upon arriving at the store, one of the grown-ups left our group to get the clothing essentials we'd need during the winter. The other two stayed with us.

As we were taken to and fro throughout the store in search of presents, I was asked by a young husband and wife what I'd like to get for

Christmas? My question, *"Can I get anything?"* might have seemed a bit impertinent or even impolite to those who were there to serve me but, if so, they never let on. When they answered *"Yes,"* I immediately found what I'd been mentally drooling over. It was a small, acrylic, paint-by-numbers set for ages 12 and up. I remember the age grouping because the lady helping me mentioned it at least twice. The second time she asked me about my proficiency at oil painting she inquired, *"Sweetheart, are you sure you can do this, it says for boys ages twelve or more and you're only eight?"* It was then that I truly realized what she was asking and was able to give her a reasonable answer.

"No, Ma'am, I can't do these pictures but my momma can and she really likes doing them. This is what I want to get her for Christmas." She objected kindly, *"But, this is supposed to be for you..."* I nodded my head and smiled as if what she and I were saying were one and the same, *"I know. This is what I want my present to be but I want to get it for my Mom. Painting makes her happy."*

In my mind, the issue was settled. If they wanted me to receive a present that would make me happy, then the paint-by-numbers set was it. Period. End of discussion.

Maybe it was my determination or the fact that I'd been continuously nodding my head up and down in a manner that declared, *"Yep, this is what we've been looking for all along"* or maybe it was just that the man and woman with me understood that Christmas simply wouldn't be Christmas if I weren't able to get my mother a wonderful present. Whatever the case might have been, that night I was able to wrap-up a 25-cent paint-by-numbers set for my mom.

Honestly, I don't remember a single item I personally received that Christmas although the small tree that dazzled us on Christmas morning seemed packed to the hilt with gifts.

While I don't remember the names of the man or woman, I do, however vaguely, remember their faces. More than anything though, I remember the way they helped me feel. I remember and cherish the fact that they took the time to enter into a young boy's heart to see what was important

110

to him and then to help him deliver a Christmas present that he would never forget. It's been nearly 40 years since that happened and the memory has never faded.

The wonderful people who came to our house that cold Christmas Eve were 'Living Jesus Out Loud' and they planted the seed of Servant Evangelism in the heart of a little boy who would grow into the man who is the author of this book today. I thank God they chose to be His hands and feet and were truly great ambassadors for Christ.

Being an ambassador for Jesus is something ALL Christians are called to be. 2 Corinthians 5:20a reads: *"We are therefore Christ's ambassadors, as though God were making his appeal through us."*

Note that the Apostle Paul was inspired to use the terms 'we' and 'us.' These small two-letter words, are inclusive of all and exclusive of none. It means 'ALL Christian's are Christ's ambassadors' – not just a select few. I mention this because there are so many people who live lives that seem to cry out in desperation – *"Help me… please!"*

As His ambassador are you willing to be there for those He's put in your path?

Chapter 14

How I Came To Know Jesus As My Savior

If you've read the earlier chapters you already know I studied with the Jehovah's Witnesses for several years until I was asked to leave the Kingdom Hall I had attended. This a continuation of my personal testimony.

Before I was asked to leave the ranks of the Jehovah's Witnesses – with whom I'd served for over three years – I began to be seriously disturbed by much of what I was being taught. This caused me to begin a serious quest for information about 'god.' As such, I began looking at every major faith I could find. This search intensified after I left the relative comfort of the Kingdom Hall – especially since their actions towards me had led to my conviction that Christianity was a crock!

In the intervening year or so after being effectively disfellowshipped (although I was never baptized as a Jehovah's Witness) I looked into Mormonism, Islam, Buddhism, Taoism (pronounced: Daoism or Dowism), Atheism, and at least a half-dozen other 'isms.' I found each one to be wanting – some more than others.

A few months after my twenty-first birthday I was approached by Ray Whitley and he wanted to talk with me about the Bible and God. I'd known Ray for few years and I respected him because he seemed to be genuine in his faith and friendly.

Over the years Ray had the opportunity to minister to me in different ways. He mowed my lawn for me when I was sick; he and his wife took me to work occasionally (when my vehicles broke down); he helped me work on my house without being asked (he'd just show-up with tools in hand and begin working); and he even picked me up once when I had drank a bit more alcohol than I should have. But, more than anything else, I respected Ray because he lived out the faith he claimed to have.

Other than knowing he was a Missionary Baptist minister (with Masters degrees in both Hebrew and Greek – something I definitely respected) who had been married nearly fifty years and who didn't believe in smoking, drinking, using foul language and about a dozen other things I considered to be a normal part of life, I didn't know much about Ray's private life. In other words, I knew Ray about as well as most of us know those who live around us. Still, because he lived out his faith, when he finally asked me to talk to him I was willing to humor him – somewhat.

In reality, I had planned on allowing Ray to get started in on his system of belief and then I was going to shut him down with my canned and highly practiced questions – questions I knew most Christians had very little knowledge about and would usually show that I was intellectually superior to them (yeah, I know… BIG EGO!).

As Ray and I began to talk he told me he believed Jesus was God, the Trinity was real and if I didn't believe what the Bible said about accepting Jesus as my Savior I'd go to Hell for eternity. Of course, I had already learned this type of belief was complete malarkey from studying Watchtower Bible and Tract Society literature but I let him continue until it was my turn to ask a couple of questions.

I asked a series of three questions, all of which were science-based and none of which I'd ever had a so-called Christian be able to answer. Many had attempted an answer but they all failed miserably to address even the most rudimentary elements of what I was inquiring about. Ray threw me for a loop when he looked at me with the most serious expression I'd ever seen him have said, *"Lonnie, I have no idea how to answer what you're asking."*

I didn't know it at the time but I'm convinced God had set me up to have Ray, a country preacher, show me the truth of His Word. Instead of arguing with me or trying to come up with an answer to my questions, Ray began asking me questions in terms that I could accept. Our conversation went something like this:

Ray: *"Do you think there's a possibility that a god exists?"*

Me: *"Sure, there's a possibility."*

Ray: *"Do you think it's possible that if a god exists that He is the One talked about in the Bible?"*

Me: *"Yeah, it's possible."*

Ray: *"Okay, is it possible that if the God of the Bible exists that He could have caused the Bible to be written so people like you and I would be able to know Him?"*

Me: *"Sure."*

Ray: *"Then, is it possible that if God caused the Bible to be written do you think it's possible He could communicate to you through His Word?"*

At this point I thought I was seeing where he was going with the conversation but I decided to play along and agreed it was possible if God existed He could communicate to us through the Bible.

Ray: *"Lonnie, have you ever read the New Testament?"*

Me: *"Yeah, of course. I studied with the Jehovah's Witnesses for over three years and we always read through the New Testament using the Watchtower and Awake magazines."*

Ray: *"No. What I'm asking is… have you ever personally read through the entire New Testament – from Matthew to Revelation – without using any type of study guide."*

I thought about it for a few seconds and said, *"No."*

Ray: *"Then I've got a challenge for you. You see, I believe that God communicates to those who seek Him through His Bible. I want you to read through the New Testament, by yourself, and, before you start, I want you to pray a prayer something like this: 'God, if you're real then when I'm reading through your Bible, reveal yourself to me.' Then, after you've finished the book of Revelation I want you to pray something like this: 'God, I've read your Bible so if you're real, reveal yourself to me through what I've just read.' Lonnie, if you'll do this, regardless of what you tell me God does or doesn't reveal to you, I'll never bring up my faith or any religion to you again. But, I'll still be your friend. Agreed?"*

I thought about Ray's challenge and I could only see positives – if I read through the New Testament and still didn't believe God existed Ray wouldn't hold it against me but, if something was revealed to me, I'd not only have a new revelation I'd still have Ray as a friend. Frankly, I didn't want to lose Ray as a friend so I said '*Yes*' more out of a desire not to hurt his feelings than anything else. But, I also knew that he'd ask me questions about what I was reading so I knew I had to read all 27 books.

That evening I prayed the prayer (or something similar) Ray had suggested and began reading the book of Matthew. Two days later I finished the book of Revelation. I never prayed the prayer he'd suggested after finishing Revelation. Instead, having read the entire New Testament, I'd become convinced God was real, Jesus was God, the Trinity was true and my eternal fate was contingent upon my acceptance or rejection of Jesus as my Savior.

Then in the early morning hours, all by myself, I asked Jesus to be my Savior. I told God I knew I had sinned and I knew I needed His Son to be in my life or else I'd go to Hell. I also told Him if He had really done all I thought He had for me, based on what I'd just read, that I'd spend the rest of my life learning as much about the Bible as I possibly could so I could answer questions for people such as myself.

I didn't really know if I had prayed correctly or not but I noticed, over the course of the next several months, major changes in my life – changes I wasn't consciously trying to make. I also knew I had an overwhelming desire to keep up my end of the bargain (believe me... salvation is most certainly a 'bargain' – *we exchange our sins for His sinlessness, our death for His life and our captivity for His freedom*).

The result of Ray's challenge to me is that I'm a forgiven man, free to love others in a way I never imagined was possible. More than this, I am now willing to be used as His hands and feet in the here now. In short, I've been adopted from a life in which I was a child of Satan into a life where I am a son of the King of Kings and I'm one of His ambassadors.

The importance of the fact we're called His ambassadors hasn't escaped me. An ambassador is the highest representative of a country in a foreign land. Their primary responsibility is to represent wishes of the head of their country in a respectful and positive manner. In short, an ambassador is the face of the Leader of whatever country they represent. If we are called to be God's ambassadors the question then becomes, *"How do we accomplish this monumental task?"*

How do you comfort the man whose wife of 53 years just breathed her last earthly breath as he held her hand; or the woman who has been abused by every man (from her father to her last boyfriend) she's ever had the displeasure of having a relationship with; or the child who lays crying in a hospital room after having been raped; or the mother who has just been told that her only two children were killed earlier in the evening by a drunk driver who survived the crash without a scratch; or the wife who has to tell her unsuspecting husband that he's got Stage IV cancer;

117

or the family who has lost everything and is now either inside or beside dumpsters when it's too hot or too cold to live inside their car?

What can you possibly say to minimize this type of suffering without also minimizing the overwhelming pain of the tragedy? Is it even possible to verbalize anything (from a Scripture to a heartfelt sympathy) that doesn't come across as completely cliché?

After years of ministering to people who have found themselves in these situations and worse, I can tell you that words will often fail to comfort. But, I can assure you that a loving attitude – whether it's through a hug, a tender touch of your hand on theirs or just sitting beside them when they have no one else to do so – will never go unnoticed or unappreciated. But, be aware that if you're going to show this type of compassion – a compassion born out of true love for others based on your relationship with Jesus – you will *sometimes* be misunderstood, abused and held in contempt. Still, if you're not 'loving on' people for show, my experience has been that your ambassadorship will shine through and the impact you'll make will be rewarded both temporally (on this side of Heaven) and eternally (in Heaven).

An example of being His ambassador is shown in the following story. The events took place in a waiting room of a hospital at about 1:30 a.m. as I was waiting to see a young lady who had tried to commit suicide.

Chapter 15

Waiting Room Evangelism

I'd left the uncomfortable chair I'd been sitting in to go to the bathroom. When I returned to the waiting room there were four African American men sitting together about three chairs away from me. They were talking in sort of hushed tones but, because the corner we were sitting in was L-shaped, I could hear every word they said.

I'd already met Robert and Lee (two older black men who were there because Lee's wife was having trouble with her heart). The other two guys I'd never seen but, because of the way they were sitting 'towards' Robert and Lee I assumed they all knew one another.

As I listened, I heard the youngest of the group (whose name I later found out was Carl) tell Robert and Lee about his concerns. I must have missed the first part of the conversation because the part I came in on went something like this:

"You know, my cousin just got sent to prison because he was selling crack. I've gotta tell you that I'm thinking about selling marijuana because the 'hit' you take on that

isn't as bad in jail time as it is for selling crack."

I was shocked that someone was actually talking, *in public*, about going into the business of selling drugs! Nonchalantly I touched the record button on my phone and began listening more intently.

Robert spoke, *"Son, don't do that. I was a principle and a school administrator for nearly thirty years and I can tell you that if you get a felony on your record it'll follow you for the rest of your life and it'll ruin most of your life. It'll be very hard for you to get a job."*

Carl continued, *"I know it sir but I don't have much of a choice. I've got two kids, my wife ran off with some other guy because I can't support us, I haven't been able to find a job in over a year and we're all living with my mother. My mom has already raised me and it's not fair that she's having to take care of me and my kids."*

"You know," Carl continued. *"I don't understand what God's doing! I go to church every week, I pay tithes on the odd jobs I get every week but it don't seem like He gives a [darn] about me! I mean, my mom was in the hospital a few months ago with congestive heart failure and my daughter just got out of the hospital a few weeks ago with a really bad infection that the doctors didn't even know what it was. Plus, Steve's sister* [he nodded to the young man on his right who was covered from head to ankles with tattoos and was looking extremely pensive and agitated], *he's my cousin and his sister was just brought in here tonight because she was attacked by three people who maced her, beat her up and stole all her stuff. I just don't understand God."*

Lee asked, *"Is everyone okay?"*

"Yeah," Carl answered. *"My mom's heart doctor told her that he didn't know why but she no longer had anything wrong with her heart and my daughter started feeling so good the next day after she was in the hospital that they let her go. One of the doctors said that she'd made a miraculous recovery. They said that Shamika* [the girl who had been attacked] *was going to be okay too."*

At this point, I had a decision to make. I could have continued to sit there, pretending to get or receive texts on my phone or I could interrupt and add my two cents into the conversation. Truly the only hesitancy on my part was that there were a room full of people and I was going to have to talk fairly loudly in order to converse with the four gentlemen. I decided it was worth being a bit uncomfortable.

I sat my phone down, took my hat off and turned towards the men. Leaning forward, to get their attention focused on me, I began…

"Guys, I know you don't know me but I'm a pastor."

Robert, at that point, smiled and said, *"Thank God."*

After asking what Carl's name was I continued, *"Carl, I heard you saying that you went to church and that you paid your tithes every week."* He nodded. *"Well, let me commend you on doing that because those are two fine things to do. We need to go to church and to honor God with the blessings He gives us but let me also tell you that you can't buy God's love. He really does love you and it doesn't matter if you ever go to church or ever give Him back a cent of what He's given you. I promise you that He is <u>for</u> you."*

"Sir, I just don't see it."

"Okay, maybe I can help you there. You said that your mom and your daughter were sick but now they're better, right?" He nodded affirmatively. *"Well, doesn't that show he cares about you and your family? Plus, I think this is a divine appointment and I'll tell you why. Just this morning, I got a call from a friend who works for a local company that is going to be hiring a LOT of people in January. They're taking applications now so if you'll give me a call and talk to me and I think that you're on the up and up I'll recommend you and I'll have my friend recommend you and, because of your size* (Carl is a BIG guy – about 6' 3" and 280 pounds – linebacker big), *I'd almost guarantee you can get hired. Now, I've got to tell you it's hot, hard work but it pays good and the guy I know who works there has been doing it for over a decade."*

Carl piped up, *"I don't care how hot it is or how hard it is, I'll work."*

"Great, let me give you one of my cards," At that point I handed a 99 for 1

Ministries card to each one of the men. *"If you don't mind emailing me your resume I'll look it over and I'll email or call you with the name of my friend."*

I turned to Steve after asking his name. *"Steve, I can see it in your body language that you're very angry and that you want revenge on whomever it was who attacked your sister."*

"[Darn] straight I do!" He replied, looking directly into my eyes.

"Well, let me give you a piece of advice. I used to be like you. I wanted revenge for just about everything. But at five feet three inches tall and 125 pounds it wasn't a good idea to look for it."

At this everyone except Steve laughed. I continued, *"Listen, I can't tell you what to do but, if I were you, I wouldn't go after the people who did this to Shamika. Do you know who it was?"*

"[Heck] yeah, got pictures of 'em doing it."

At this point Robert interjected, *"Then boy, go to the cops and force them to do their job. Don't you go getting yourself thrown in jail just because you're [ticked] off."*

"I agree Steve," I said. *"In fact, one of the security guards here at this hospital is an officer. Could I get him to come and talk to you."*

After a few minutes he agreed and I motioned for the guard to join us. The guard took down pertinent information and promised to contact Steve and Shamika once he found anything.

Sensing I'd done everything I could and feeling that God wanted to speak to our hearts I asked, *"Listen guys, would you mind if I prayed for all of you?"*

At that point I knelt on the floor between them, felt every eye in the room on me (I was the only white person in the waiting room), took all of their hands into my own and prayed.

Later that evening Carl emailed me his resume. I found out he was only a couple of semester's shy of getting his Bachelor's degree (he had to stop going to school because he lost his job and couldn't afford the tuition). Steve reported the three people who had attacked his sister and they were taken into custody and Shamika is doing great.

A few days later I got a call from Carl and this is what he told me. *"Pastor Lonnie, when you first started talking to us in the waiting room I just thought you were some crazy little white guy who wanted to butt in and read me the riot act. The fact that you talked to us with such respect, prayed for us and gave me a hug... well, that's the nicest thing a white person has ever done for me."*

Folks, I gotta tell you... it hurt me to know that a simple prayer and a hug was the nicest thing a white person had ever done for Carl.

That's crazy! We should ALL be out there loving on everyone possible – regardless of their skin color, how many tattoos they have or how badly they smell.

This just goes to show you that sharing God's love, even in the middle of a waiting room, pays off!

As you read the preceding story you probably noticed that I didn't bother quoting Scripture to those I was ministering to. While I don't think there would have been anything wrong in doing so, I was simply led to put the love of Jesus into action rather than just talking about the love He has for all of us.

A great ending to this story is that Carl went for an interview, got hired and has been working for the company I referred him to for over a year now. His children are doing well, he finally graduated and is in line for a promotion and he's in the process of purchasing his first house.

This young man still struggles from time to time but he's learned to turn to other Christians for support and, in his own words,

"I never knew Jesus was real until He showed Himself to me through all the

Christians I wasn't paying any attention to before. Now, Jesus and I are tight! I know that He loves me and my family and it's not because of anything I do but just because He does!"

Steve, Carl's cousin, went to jail for a brief stint after turning himself in for a crime he'd committed a few months prior to our meeting but was let out early for good behavior. Today, he's working alongside Carl, is attending a local college and is very active in the youth ministry of the church he attends.

If you are a Christian, my advice to you is to always remember that we're here on this earth for a tiny, fraction of a millisecond in comparison to eternity and since we are all dying, from the moment we're born, you should learn make each moment count by learning to live as though you are going to spend eternity with or without those you come in contact with because you will.

So, do what we were taught to do in kindergarten:

Show [people that Jesus loves them] and Tell [people the good news of the Gospel]!

Chapter 16

Are You Willing to Be a Seed Flinger?

Jesus Himself likened His own Kingdom to that of a seed which is planted inside the hearts of mankind. I'm convinced beyond the shadow of a doubt that every person, be they born in a Christ-rich or Christ-barren environment, is given an opportunity cultivate the seed of Jesus' Kingdom or, conversely to discard it completely.

According to the Joshua Project (a Christian project dedicated to evangelizing those who don't yet know about Christ), there are almost 3 billion people who have not yet heard the Gospel. But, without a doubt, it is up to God to draw people to Him if there are no Christians who are with them to be His hands and feet.

Approximately 20 years ago I had the opportunity to hear Kamau speak at a church in Texas. I had no idea what to expect because I didn't know anything about Kamau except that he was a missionary to the African nation.

As it turned out, Kamau's story is one I've been able to repeat over and over again when a person raises the objection that '*It wouldn't be fair for God to send anyone to Hell to whom He has not revealed Himself.*'

Obviously, the following story is paraphrased (I was a very young Christian at the time and didn't have the foresight to tape the meeting and the church has since undergone radical changes (the original elderly pastor has died and the church itself has moved locations) so there is no one I know of who has a recording), but I'll tell it the same way I've told it hundreds of times before.

Kamau was born and raised in the interior of Africa. It was so far removed from anything we'd call civilization he'd never even seen an airplane in the skies under which he lived. In broken and heavily accented English He told everyone in attendance about how he came to give His life to Jesus.

The Story of Kamau

"I grew up in a village where we were taught to worship the sun and moon and even animals. I remember as a young boy taking offerings of food, woven baskets filled with trinkets made of wood and rock, herbs and other things and placing them before totem poles and on rocks and even burying things in the ground in an attempt to gain favor or appease the gods we thought brought everything from rain, wind, crop growth and even the sunrise.

From the time I was a young man (I don't know how old I was then or even how old I am even today because we didn't have birth certificates), I began questioning our elders as to the reasons behind our religious traditions. I was told it wasn't appropriate to question what we did for the gods and, in short, if I didn't stop my questions I could cause these gods to bring judgment upon our entire village. That stopped me from openly questioning the reasons behind what we did but I remember lying outside at night, looking up at the stars, and, secretly, asking myself if what we did made sense.

Eventually, I began to seriously watch the seasons and how our crops reacted to our offerings. There seemed to be no rhyme or reason to what happened. Sometimes it would rain for days and destroy what we'd planted and, at other times, it would be so dry that our crops would die from lack of water. The men and women in our village died from attacks by beasts or some of them would simply waste away.

The thing that bothered me the most is that at the base of the totem poles the things we'd leave for our gods would either rot, be eaten by wild animals or whisked away by the winds and other elements. From what I'd seen, if it had not been for the natural processes of decay or scavengers, the food and other gifts we presented to our gods would have never gone away. This caused a conflict in my mind because I'd been told stories from the time I was a small child of the gods who would come and feast upon our sacrifices. It simply didn't happen and, as I grew older, I watched and saw it was a lie.

Eventually, I became convinced that while there had to be something or someone 'bigger' than us that whatever it happened to be it wasn't found in a totem pole or a rock or in the ground.

I became restless and would wander around our village like a madman searching for answers to my questions. I remember dancing for hours on end, until I thought my body was going to simply drop from exhaustion and I remember drinking a special mixture that was supposed to help us commune with our gods. Nothing ever happened for me.

I was truly desperate to know why I existed and why all these things happened to my friends and family and I began to talk to no one and nothing in particular, asking always to be given a vision of the true god, if there was one. I didn't know what I was doing is called prayer here in America but that's what I was doing. I was praying to a god I didn't know even existed.

For a long time, I don't know how long, I tried going about my daily life as if everything was okay but I noticed that many, many of my friends and family were keeping their distance from me. I had become strange to them.

Finally, one night as I slept, I had a dream of a strange village far away from my own home. When I awoke from my sleep I remembered the village and something told me to go to it. Honestly, I tried to discount the dream because I'd never seen such a strange village before and I instinctively knew that it was several days journey away from my own. But, I couldn't get rid of the dream and the more I tried talking myself out of going the more I began to realize it wasn't going to go away until I tried to find the village I'd seen.

I decided I had to try to find the village I'd dreamt of. So, with nothing but a 'sense of direction' as to where I should walk, I struck out one night after most everyone in my village was asleep. I decided to travel at night, despite the fact I might encounter wild animals, because I knew, within a day or two, I'd possibly encounter hostile tribes. So, for three nights I walked, as quickly and as quietly as possible, through the vast wilderness that is my homeland. When I'd see a village in the distance I'd avoid it by walking as far away as I thought was necessary not to be noticed by anyone who might live there. I slept during the day, covering myself with grass I'd gather just before sunrise. It wasn't an easy sleep and I was quickly becoming weaker because I had to find plants to eat and get water from.

In the early morning on the third day I saw a village in the distance and, somehow, I knew this was where I was supposed to go. I approached very cautiously. As I grew closer to the village I began to see markings I'd dreamed of. While this excited me I was also very concerned because I didn't know what most of the symbols meant.

The huts in this village were much better constructed than those in my own village and there were tracks in the sand that didn't look like any animal could have made them. Still, I pressed into the village. Even though I could hear the blood rushing in my ears and I thought the beating of my heart was so loud it would certainly bring attention to me, it was as if I were compelled to keep going.

Thankfully, no one in the village seemed to be awake. I eventually came upon a wooden hut that had steps leading up to a door. I climbed the steps and, suddenly, I felt as though I had to stop. I stopped and waited. I waited and waited and waited. Nothing. No one came to the door. Eventually my heart stopped beating so rapidly and I sat down on the steps. Fatigue overcame me and, even though I was still scared, I fell into a light sleep.

The next thing I knew I heard the door open behind me and, before I could rise, I felt a hand on my shoulder. I looked at the fingers and they were pale. I quickly turned my head towards the arm that held the fingers and, for the first time in my life, I saw a white man. I almost vomited. I wanted so badly to run but my legs wouldn't lift my body from the sitting position.

The white man was looking at me… more like he was studying me. I didn't realize it at the time but what he was doing was looking at the markings on my skin. Then he did something I never expected… he spoke to me in my language. It wasn't perfectly 'my' language but it was close enough I knew he and I would be able to talk. After my initial shock, I realized there were others who had the same skin color as me standing behind him. That's when I became very scared. He must have noticed the fright on my face because he smiled and said a word I understood as meaning 'your friends.'

As I found my voice, I began to tell this white man who I was and that I didn't know why I'd come to his village except that I'd had a dream in which I was told to come here to find out answers about a god. He smiled even wider and, for the first time in my life, I heard the name Jesus.

Soon enough I found out he was a missionary from a Baptist church who had come to my country to tell everyone about Jesus the Christ. After only a few days I accepted Jesus as my Savior and my God – the ONLY TRUE GOD! [Kamau shouted this.] Now, after I'd returned to my village with this white man and others, my people no longer sacrifice to idols. Instead, they love the God who made them – The Father, The Son

129

and The Holy Spirit!"

I have attempted to relate Kamau's story with as few embellishments as possible because I want you to know that if a person is truly seeking God I believe He can and will reveal Himself to them – even if it's through a vision or an encounter with a missionary. In other words, God's love can reach anyone!

Still, I also believe, for the most part, God uses us as His stewards because each of us has the seed of the kingdom within us (seed we're expected to scatter broadly – not keep to ourselves). If we're faithful to distribute the seeds He's given to us then we know that He'll be faithful to bring those seeds that find good soil (hearts that are ready and willing to accept His Son) to fruition. We're told as much in Jesus' Parable of the Sower in Matthew 13:1-8 (TLB).

"... *Jesus left the house and went down to the shore, where an immense crowd soon gathered. He got into a boat and taught from it while the people listened on the beach. He used many illustrations such as this one in his sermon: 'A farmer was sowing grain in his fields. As he scattered the seed across the ground, some fell beside a path, and the birds came and ate it. And some fell on rocky soil where there was little depth of earth; the plants sprang up quickly enough in the shallow soil, but the hot sun soon scorched them and they withered and died, for they had so little root. Other seeds fell among thorns, and the thorns choked out the tender blades. But some fell on good soil and produced a crop that was thirty, sixty, and even a hundred times as much as he had planted.*"

Jesus' disciples were often just as baffled by His parables as the huge crowds of people who came to hear Him preach. This one was no different so when he was alone with them, He explained the Parable of the Sower in plain language:

"*Now here is the explanation of the story I told about the farmer planting grain: The hard path where some of the seeds fell represents the heart of a person who hears the Good News about the Kingdom and doesn't understand it; then Satan comes and snatches away the seeds from his heart. The shallow, rocky soil represents the heart of a man who hears the message and receives it with real joy, but he doesn't have much depth in his life, and the seeds don't root very deeply, and after a while when trouble comes, or persecution begins because of his beliefs, his enthusiasm fades, and he drops out. The ground covered with thistles represents a man who hears the message, but the cares of this life and his longing for money choke out God's Word, and he does less and less for God. The good ground represents the heart of a man who listens to the message and understands it and goes out and brings thirty, sixty, or even a hundred others into the Kingdom."*

My question to you is: Will you become a 'seed flinger?' Are you willing to do what Jesus commanded all of His followers to do and share the love of God with everyone – to the ends of the earth (which includes your next door neighbors, the person living on the street, little children, the elderly and, of course, those in countries who have yet to hear, personally, the Word of God)?

There are two reasons I ask this question:

1) I want you to know the Great Commission commands us to do exactly what I just proposed (Matthew 28:16-20).

2) I want you to recognize the Kingdom of God is within YOU and YOU have the full authority, power and commission, from God, to speak His Word to all who'll listen and even to those who won't (Luke 17:20-21).

Knowing this… are you willing to go out into the highways, byways and hedges to invite people of every skin color, every language and from every walk of life, to accept The Way, The Truth and The Life (Jesus) into their own lives?

If not, I suggest that you reconsider your salvation or, at the very least, ask that God grant you the courage to live for Him regardless of how uncomfortable doing so makes you.

Chapter 17

SPECIAL SECTION: OUTREACH STORIES AND IDEAS

Responding To An Unanswerable Question

A few years ago I was part of a team of Christians who had volunteered to help a family rebuild their home in the aftermath of Katrina. A television crew was roaming the area looking for 'human interest' stories and they happened upon our ragtag crew. As the only minister who was on the scene I was asked if I'd mind being interviewed.

The very first thing I was asked was a 'gotcha question.' In other words, the reporter knew I wouldn't have any type of intelligent answer.

"*So,*" the reporter began. "*Pastor Honeycutt, the question I'm certain everyone is asking, in the aftermath of the hurricane that has devastated the lives of so many people, including your own friends, is 'why?' Why does God allow this kind of event to take place?*"

Without thinking I gave her the following answer, "*I don't know. But, what*

I do know is how God wants us to respond to tragedies like this. He wants us, as Christians, to show up and help whomever we can. There was a lot of tragedy when Jesus walked on the earth and He never solved problems en masse. Instead, what He did was minister to individuals. That's what I believe we're called to do as well."

She was so shocked by my answer I wasn't asked any other questions. Instead, the reporter and the cameraman left me and went to the next house. About an hour later I saw the reporter and cameraman packing up to go to their next assignment. I smiled and waved and the reporter walked over to me and said,

"In all the years I've been reporting I've never had any preacher not try to defend the actions of God. Why didn't you?"

I smiled, laughed a little and said, *"Because I'm not God. I have no idea why He allows things like this to happen. All I know is that when they do He wants us to help pick up the pieces. Maybe it's His way of drawing us together. I honestly don't know."*

"Hmm," was all she said before turning, getting in the news van and leaving.

That night everyone who had been present when I was interviewed watched the news report. The report was ten minutes long (an incredibly long report for local news) but my comments didn't appear at any time. I wasn't surprised.

In my youth I tried to answer every objection anyone raised about God or His Word. I learned that attempting to give answers for which you have little or no true insight simply makes both parties highly agitated with each other. As I've matured, I've given up trying to respond to questions to which only God knows the answers. Instead, I've learned, through trial and error, to answer questions to which I know there is a proper response. That God led me to give the answer I did was confirmed when, about eight months later, the reporter and I recognized each other at an outdoor event. She was off-duty and we chatted about this and that until she finally said:

"Pastor, I want to thank you for the answer you did __not__ give me about 'why God would allow tragedies.' You planted a seed in my heart that really made me think about things I've questioned most of my life and your answer made a lot of sense to me. I want you to know that I've begun going to a Messianic Jewish congregation and I'm really having a lot of fun helping people Yeshua Yahweh is putting in our path."

Seed flinging is an occupation for every Christian.

The job is simple: Sow seeds of Christ's influence wherever you are and as often as possible. There are a myriad of ways to fling the seeds of the Gospel. Of course, the number one way to influence the growth of a crop of Christians is to live out the life Jesus not only expects you to but commands you to.

Again, by living Jesus out loud (following His commands and not just giving verbal ascent to them), you'll not only show people Jesus is a good example for life, you'll also be training those who follow in your footsteps the most natural form of evangelization available.

However, while I believe that living Jesus out loud is the best way to introduce people to Jesus, there are times, once a person has been attracted to Jesus through your life, you'll need visual, audio and other demonstrable tools to draw them closer to Him and to illustrate why it is that your life reflects values other than the ones the world (pre-Christians) hold near and dear. With this in mind, I encourage you to use as many forms of seed flinging (tracts, parties, megaphones, outdoor concerts, etc.) as you're led to try.

A Few Ideas for Seed Flinging

The following is a partial list of the ways I have flung seed with my ministry. If you find any seed flinging method that captures your attention and you'd like more information on it (or you'd like to share some with us), please don't hesitate to contact us:

99 for 1 Ministries
P.O. Box 180932
Mobile, AL. 36618
www.99for1ministries.com

[Keep in mind that what I've listed is meant to get your creative juices flowing – to show that God can work even in the midst of Christians doing weird stuff.]

Handing Out Christian Tracts

I know what you're thinking… tracts are SO old fashioned. However, done right, tracts can be an extremely effective tool for introducing people to a concept or doctrine they may have questions about. This, in turn, can lead to 'Old Fashioned' techniques of talking and Bible study.

We might do well to remember that cults, such as the Jehovah's Witnesses distribute millions of tracts every week in the U.S. alone. Since their numbers are increasing it may be that someone, somewhere is finding a tract that attracts their attention enough to get them to call their local Kingdom Hall for a Free 'Bible' study.

For a list of FREE Tracts you can print out from your own computer go to:

http://www.padfield.com/downloads/tracts.html

For ideas on using any and all tracts see:

http://www.biblebelievers.com/Torrey3.html

Remember: There's no cookie-cutter tract that's good for everyone on every level. If at all possible you'll want to be aware of the person's needs, wants and desires before giving them a tract. Everyone has different personalities, interests and outlooks on life including, but not limited to, previous religious instruction, family structures, lifestyles, educational levels and different dynamics in their lives such as divorce, death, birth, marriage and age. But, as long as the tract you hand out contains the truth of God's Word and is actually read we've got a promise from God Himself that His Word will not go out and come back empty. It WILL produce fruit.

Tracts, as with all forms of evangelization, are simply a bridge building tool – not a be-all and end-all method of salvation.

Golf Cart Rides

Escorting someone to or from their car into a supermarket, mall, flea market (wherever) is definitely a soft touch way of entering into a person's life but I guarantee they'll remember it.

Almost everyone, but especially the elderly, will really appreciate the kindness of someone offering a ride on a golf cart to and from their vehicle when it's very hot, very cold or raining. A ride on a golf cart is extremely fun for kids and parents will appreciate the help getting their children wherever they're going safely.

One year, around Thanksgiving and Christmas, we rented two, six-person, covered golf carts went to the mall and began roaming the parking lot in search of any and everyone who wanted a ride to and from their vehicle.

We put a very visible sign on the front of the cart that read: **FREE RIDES!**

Most people thought we were part of the mall staff. Every time we were at the mall security guards would eventually approach us and ask us who we were. We'd say something like, *'We're just a Christian Church who thought we'd come out and help people get to and from your shops – no strings attached.'* We'd usually give them one of our outreach cards so they'd know we really weren't charging anyone anything.

One time I had to talk to the mall manager but she was more than happy to allow us to help her customers – especially since it was seen as a positive community touch.

As we drove people to the mall we had a couple of minutes to introduce ourselves and to hand our passengers a 'goody bag' that held the following:

1. Our 'No Strings Attached' business card (just in case they happened to lose the one we gave our passengers).
2. A couple of pieces of sugar-free chewing gum.
3. Two coupons for a free ice cream from Chic-Fil-A (we've used Chic-Fil-A as a 'go to' source for coupons for years – they're usually more than happy to know we'll be handing out hundreds of coupons promoting their business).
4. Individually wrapped pieces of candy (hard candy works best when it's hot because it doesn't melt easily but, when it's cold we usually splurge and get carmels, chocolates, etc.).

To show you how much fun people can have helping others, even when the weather has been terrible (raining, sleeting or very hot), we've always had more volunteers than we've had time to use. In fact, every time we did this particular outreach, those who participated wanted to do it again and had told others who practically begged to get a spot as a driver.

Umbrella Escorts

Umbrellas are items most people don't have when they need them the most. By being aware of your local forecast, you can be a hero to the elderly and moms with kids who find it difficult to make it from stores to their cars in the rain. When entering a store, men and teenage boys have a tendency to simply plow through the rain regardless of how badly it's pouring. However, when they're coming out of a store and are either carrying items or pushing a cart, most of them are very thankful to have someone standing by with an umbrella.

Of course, rain isn't the only time an umbrella escort is appropriate. Some areas are so sunny and hot that umbrellas can provide relief (especially to older people and those with babies).

Regardless of the weather, I suggest you go in pairs (one male, one female is the best scenario because guys always look less intimidating with a woman beside them) and take two golf-sized umbrellas with you. This allows you and your partner to either walk beside the person(s) you're escorting or it allows the person you're helping to carry an umbrella (some people are very peculiar about personal space) while you talk with them.

Keeping personal health in mind, if it's raining I suggest you dress in a water proof poncho and galoshes and, if it's very hot, I suggest a hat, sun screen and shorts and lots of water.

Since escorting someone with an umbrella requires rather close quarters I suggest that you either chew gum or keep and use mouthwash *often*. This may seem like a minor detail but people are really turned off when you're trying to talk to them and you have bad breath (whether from eating and not being able to brush your teeth or general halitosis). I can attest to this personally as I've had to hold my breath when someone who had bad breath was trying to talk to me. It's simply better to stay prepared than it is to realize you've committed a social faux pas.

Outreach Cards

Each and every person we help (over the age of 12) is given a single business card that has the following information – on BOTH the Back and Front of the card: (next page)

> **This is Our Way of Showing Jesus' Love For You in a Practical Way!**
>
> **No Strings Attached!**
>
> Name of your Church or Organization and a Contact Phone Number

The card can be in plain black and white (it reduces the cost dramatically) and it'll serve not only to validate who you are (a Christian) but will also introduce your church or organization to in a non-confrontational way.

$1 Car Wash

One of the best ways to generate interest (especially on a busy intersection) is by hosting a $1 Car Wash.

All this outreach requires is some willing, energetic hands, lots of soap, water, good old-fashioned elbow grease and signs – lots of signs!

Signs are the most important part of this outreach because they're your advertisement. Nothing fancy is needed (handmade signs are fine) but they need to be simple and readable by people going past in cars at 40 mph or faster. I prefer signs that are simple. Those that read, in **BIG, BOLD** type:

Example of a Good Sign (next page)

$1

CAR WASH

← ← ← ← ← ← ← ←

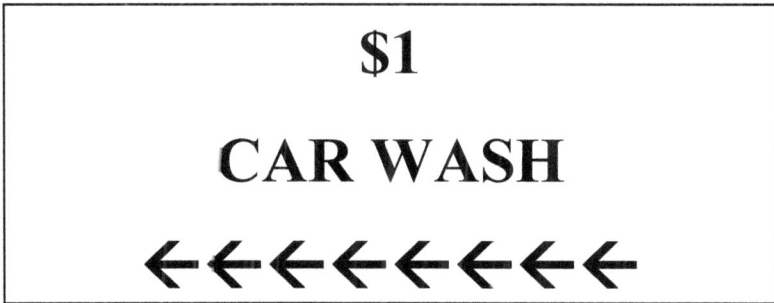

[Note: If you use arrows, make certain the person holding the sign points the arrows in the correct direction – towards the washing area and not across the street.
Yes, I've seen this happen! ☺]

The sign shown above is MUCH better than those with either SKINNY writing or too much information – you know you've seen them:

Example of a Bad Sign

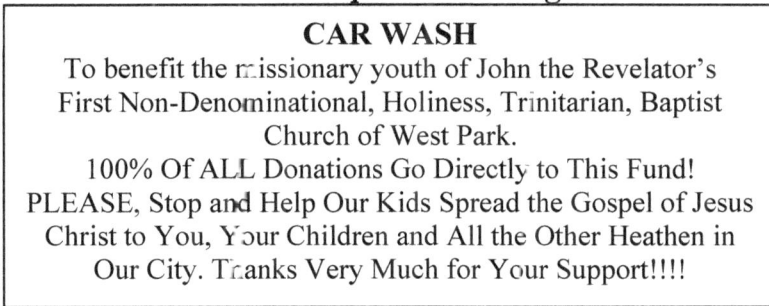

> **CAR WASH**
> To benefit the missionary youth of John the Revelator's
> First Non-Denominational, Holiness, Trinitarian, Baptist
> Church of West Park.
> 100% Of ALL Donations Go Directly to This Fund!
> PLEASE, Stop and Help Our Kids Spread the Gospel of Jesus
> Christ to You, Your Children and All the Other Heathen in
> Our City. Thanks Very Much for Your Support!!!!

Obviously the above mock-up of a sign is exaggerated but, when I see this type of sign, I just want to roll my eyes in frustration!

Why a $1 Car Wash?

In my opinion, the worst signs are those that announce, in large letters:
FREE CAR WASH!

Give me a break! Even if the sign was telling the truth, NO ONE believes it!

In fact, every time I've pulled into a car washing area after seeing a sign telling me that I could get a FREE CAR WASH, I've ALWAYS been hit-up for a donation. Even if the suggestion to give something to those washing my vehicle was subtle:

"You know, these kids are really enjoying themselves out in this heat. But, this is nothing compared to how hot it's going to be in Death Valley when they're building houses for the poor… if they can get enough money to get there."

The reason for a $1 Car Wash is simple: People know what's going to be expected for you to wash their vehicle. One dollar. That's it. It's a fixed price.

But, there will be a catch. What they aren't told by the sign is that when they pull into your car washing area they'll be given a dollar bill!

That's right… THEY will be GIVEN $1 just for letting you have the privilege of washing their vehicle.

Right away that sounds a bit bizarre doesn't it? Imagine how bizarre it'll seem to them. But, imagine being able to answer the questions they'll have such as:

"Why are you doing this?"
"What do you mean you're going to give me a dollar for washing my car?"
"I don't understand?"

I've rarely participated in any outreach that's more effective in getting the attention of people than a $1 Car Wash. It is absolutely amazing the kind of ministry that one dollar, a few energetic kids and a friendly smile can buy.

For instance, during one of the first $1 Car Washes I participated in, a lady who had just lost her husband after he'd fought a lengthy battle with cancer pulled her car into the parking lot where we'd set-up tents, fans and seats (so our customers wouldn't have to sweat while waiting).

She was escorted from her car to a seat where one of the ladies working with us took her order for a soft drink and a hotdog. She began taking a few dollars from her purse when I walked over and handed her a single dollar bill. She said, *"No. I'm sorry. I don't work here. I'm not sure who we're supposed to give our money to even."*

I laughed a bit and introduced myself. Soon after she'd accepted the dollar, her soft drink and hotdog we began to talk and she told me her name was Catherine. Another volunteer, Betty, and I found ourselves drawn to her.

Catherine had just come from a local funeral home where she'd put a down payment on the burial ceremony for her husband. At first she seemed to be taking his death in stride but, as soon as Betty leaned in and gave her a hug, the tears began flowing.

During the next 15 minutes (the time it took for her car to be washed), we learned, among other things, that she and Charles had been married just over five years. He'd been diagnosed with intestinal cancer a year after they were wed and had undergone surgery to remove nearly eighty percent of his intestines, most of his stomach and finally, his entire esophagus. Their sixth anniversary was only two months away but Charles had died three days before we met her. Making things much worse was that Catherine felt as though she'd not been a good enough wife or caretaker to her husband in the past several months. She actually blamed herself for his sudden downturn in health. It quickly became apparent to Betty and I that she didn't have anyone to talk to and probably hadn't for quite some time. When I asked her, very directly, if she went to church, had friends or family in the area or had seen a counselor before or since the death of her husband, her answer was 'No' across the board.

To make a long story short, Betty exchanged phone numbers with Catherine and I took down other pertinent information I was able to use to get a professional counselor involved in her life. I talked the situation over with one of the pastors at the car wash (I wasn't yet ordained) and, together, we called several churches in the area in which Catherine lived to make certain someone from each of them would contact her as soon as possible. In less than two weeks Catherine had begun attending two of the churches in her area and a month later had become a member of one of them. Betty and I kept up with Catherine for nearly two years until I left the area. To this day (nearly ten years later), Betty and Catherine are still in contact with one another – they go to lunch, visit hospitals and Catherine sponsors many of the outreaches the church she attends puts on.

Most of the $1 Car Washes don't end up with this type of impact but, still, you never know who you'll meet or what God will do.

Mark Wyatt, the Senior Pastor of Deeper Life Fellowship, and I once had the opportunity to pray for a sold out atheist who told us, very forthrightly, that he didn't believe in all the *"mumbo-jumbo that you Christians do."* We told him, *"That's okay, we do."* Then, this man, who had just disparaged our faith but who was looking for direction in his life, allowed two strangers to pray for him. I don't know whatever became of Sean but, regardless of whether our prayers for him were answered in the manner we prayed to God they would be, I'll guarantee he remembers all the kindness everyone at the car wash showed him.

Ministering To Those Begging on Street Corners

Note: I'm extremely safety oriented so I would advise against any woman EVER going out of the sight of others with anyone when ministering on the street. I'd also suggest that even men go in pairs when ministering to people who are homeless.

A question I'm often asked is: How can I effectively minister to those standing on the side of the road holding signs that state: 'Hungry. Need Food' or 'Homeless. Anything Helps' etc.

My first suggestion is to you pray God will put people who need help in your path because if you're willing to help them you may be the only 'Jesus' they ever see.

My second suggestion is that you take the signs that are held as being true. So, if you see someone holding a sign that states they are hungry then you should assume that food is what they're looking for. If this is true then we, as Christians, should be ready to give them what they're looking for – *food*.

My third suggestion is, whenever it's possible and safe, you take a few minutes to personally hand these folks (who are loved by Jesus) food, shake their hands or give them a hug and offer a quick (or long) prayer for them. Here's what I've found to be an effective 'kit' to keep in your vehicle (this fits in a one gallon zip-lock bag):

The $5 Food Kit

- Brunswick® Tuna Fish or Chicken Salad and Crackers or Healthy Choice® Fresh Mixers
- 1 Can of Armour® Vienna Sausages
- Chef Boyardee® Spaghetti and Meatballs
- Kraft Macaroni and Cheese® (Individual size – Microwavable)
- Small bag of Brach's® Fruit Snacks
- 1 Bottle of Water
- 1 G Series Gatorade® Powder Packs that can be added to water

When you encounter people living on the street and you want to give them food, take into consideration at least two RULES:

- Most don't have can openers.
- Most know where they can go to use a microwave and water is almost always available to them (even if it's from a sink in a restroom or fast food restaurant).

Given these rules you can probably understand why we've chosen the foods we handout on a daily basis – every container is easily accessible without a can opener (they can either be torn open or have 'pop tops') and one of the containers (the Healthy Choice) can be reused (to heat or store leftovers) if needed. If you decide to put fruit in your kit, remember it may spoil relatively quickly in warm or hot weather.

This Food Kit will cost just under $5 – especially if you buy foods like Healthy Choice meals in bulk. Feel free to mix, match or completely revamp the kit you put together – just make certain the 2 RULES are followed.

You may have noticed that the kit described had NAME BRAND food items. As of February 2012 the cost of the kit was exactly $4.92 and that's Family Dollar store shelf prices. If you know someone who uses coupons or if you want to use store brand (generic) foods, you can probably get the cost to around $4.

However, before going the cheapest route you should consider the impact of the following question:

If YOU were on the receiving end of this gift would you feel better about it if you were given name brand foods or generic brand foods?

There's obviously a trade-off. Generic foods allow you to get more food for less money. However, in my opinion, the few cents you'll save aren't as important as giving someone foods that YOU (or I) would want to eat.

This was brought to my attention when I briefly volunteered at a hospice center serving people with AIDS. I was part of a team that collected, sorted and distributed food. Invariably, every day, we'd get foods that were about to expire, had expired or that people simply didn't want to eat (asparagus, pinto beans, curry, canned squid, etc.). While there's nothing wrong with any of the aforementioned food items (with the exception of the expired ones), if you're honest, would YOU rather get a can of squid or a can of corn or even beef stew? I think the answer is obvious.

I also suggest giving those you meet <u>factory sealed foods</u> because it lessens your liability. This is much more important for ministries and/or churches but, nevertheless, it's a good idea. Homemade food, while great, has a tendency to have a MUCH shorter lifespan than do prepackaged foods. Unless you know the food is going to be consumed almost immediately (such as when you serve it to a group of people), I'd really suggest going the prepackaged route.

Keeping food kits like this available (and within reach) in your vehicle means you'll be able to minister to those you encounter without much fear that what you're giving them (as in cash) will be able to be bartered for alcohol or tobacco products. But, even if what you give them is somehow parlayed into something less than desirable, remember:

They WILL remember you – especially if you show-up every day or two and give them something nourishing.

Just as Jesus knew that there would be those who wouldn't live for Him after He healed, prayed for or fed them, He still showed His love by doing exactly that. Should we, as His followers, do any less?

Ministering To Those In Hospital Waiting Rooms

It's uncomfortable when you walk into a waiting room because you don't know why people are there. It could be a happy occasion (such as when grandparents are waiting for news that their grandchild has been born) or an occasion of grief (such as when a grandchild is waiting to hear the news that their grandparent has died). As such, unless you know those in the waiting room (or if you are an outrageously empathetic, grace and mercy-filled person), entering into the lives of those in a waiting room can be downright intimidating.

If intimidated is an adjective that describes how you'd feel going into a waiting room, I think you'll appreciate the following approach.

Pastor Mark Wyatt, has aptly stated, *"The last place most people want to be is in the waiting room of a hospital."*

With this in mind, we've created a way to make their stay a bit more pleasant while, at the same time, opening the door for possibly deep ministry.

When entering a waiting room for the purpose of ministry it's possible, even probable, for emotions to run high. While this isn't anything to be overly concerned about, it is something that everyone should be aware of. Still, none of the members of 99 for 1 Ministries (some of whom have been doing this for nearly thirty years) have EVER encountered anyone who was overtly rude. I believe this is because we're showing up under the banner of Christ's love.

Hospital Goody Bags

One of our volunteers, Greg H., explains: "I do a LOT of hospital visits. Sometimes I'll know ahead of time that I'll be going to a hospital known for long waiting room lines. Other times, I plan on taking teams of people to waiting rooms. In either case, when I walk into the room I stand at the door (sometimes holding it open for upwards of 10 or more people) and say something like: *"Hi, I'm Greg and we're from a local church. We know that the last place you probably want to be is in a hospital waiting room so, we've brought you gifts to help your wait be a bit less tedious. It's just our way of saying Jesus loves you – NO strings attached!"*

At this point, without waiting (due to the fact most of those in the waiting room are probably staring at us with either empty, questioning stares or slack jaws), we begin handing out the bags of goodies to every person.

Since we know there will often be children in the waiting rooms who are bored out of their little minds – they're used to playing games etc. but, instead, are either very hyper or extremely talkative (both of which can just about drive their parents as well as other people in the room to the brink of insanity) – we ALWAYS have special bags for the young ones.

As we hand out these goody bags we ask probing questions like:

"How long have you been waiting?"
"Who are you waiting for?"
"What type of procedure is the person you're waiting on having done?"

Once we've established we're not a bunch of nuts, we offer to pray for them and the person they're waiting for.

A word to the wise: Don't be surprised if the person you're praying with asks you to go to the room of the patient.

If this happens I've got one would of advice for you… "<u>GO</u>!"

Greg's advice is perfect and can be duplicated by practically anyone.

The Hospital Goody Bags 99 for 1 Ministries create ALWAYS contain the following:

- Small Note Pad and Pen
- Gum (Sugarless)
- Candy & Chips
- Two $1 bills (for vending machines)
- Coloring Book & Crayons
- No Strings Attached Card

The average cost for this type of Goody Bag is less than $6 and that includes the two $1 bills. If you buy things in bulk you can make a Goody Bag for under $4!

There is almost nothing more comforting for those who are in a hospital to know that there is someone (even if it's a complete stranger) they can call to talk to or to ask for help from.

We've done this so often it's not uncommon for us to encounter people who stay at a hospital for weeks at a time. Two ladies we've recently encountered had been 'living' in the waiting room where their husbands were hospitalized for two and three months respectively! You cannot believe the relief (not to mention the love) they felt when our volunteers began showing up with home-cooked meals and to simply sit and chat.

A gentleman, before he died, wrote a note to one of our volunteers that read (paraphrased): "*You know, having priests and chaplains come to my room is nice but I know they're getting paid to be nice. But you people... you people are special. You don't get paid but you still show up. No one even knows you're around but you're here. My wife and I won't ever forget you.*"

Folks, that's what Christian ministry is all about – being remembered for treating others the way we'd like to be treated.

Chapter 18

When Flinging Seed – Be Creative!

Hopefully some of what I've shared with you has opened your eyes to see the astounding array of ways you can minister the love of Christ to people. Believe me, what I've shared is the tip of the iceberg of what you can do. The sky is practically the limit. In fact, an elderly couple I recently met has taken the phrase ('the sky is the limit') and put a whole new spin on it.

Skydiving With a Higher Purpose

Both Henry and Marianna are skydiving pros. They have a 'mom and pop' ministry called 'Disguise the Limit' and it revolves around skydivers. Together they claim to have made over 13,000 jumps (not an enormous amount for some but 13,000 more than the author of this book has ever made). In the 1980's Henry began filming their jumps and was soon showing his 'movies' to friends and family. Close-up shots of distorted facial features (flapping flesh around the neck, cheeks that ballooned out) and the landings (some beautiful and some not so pretty) were soon the 'talk of the town.'

By the time the 1990's rolled around Marianna had been drawn into Henry's hobby and soon discovered that she had a penchant for computer manipulation of the videos. In the decade that followed they were filming upwards of 50% of the jumps made by first-time jumpers and selling the videos for a handsome price. According to Marianna, when a pastor and his wife came to the airport for their first jump, Henry decided he wanted her to try something a bit different. Instead of simply adding 'credits' at the beginning and the end of the video that told who was diving, flying the plane and filming, Henry wanted to add Bible verses before, during and after the jump. The next Sunday the pastor showed his congregation the film and everyone went wild. The rest, as they say, is history.

Today, due to technological advancements, Henry is able to control four small video cameras that are fitted onto each skydiver from the comfort of a small studio. He captures all the drama possible (from the initial leap and free fall to the landings) as well as all the comedy possible (from the hesitation just before a person leaps from a plane to funny facial expressions). Their grandson, who owns two airplanes and is a partner in the private airport they operate from, collects all the pertinent information from each participant (name, address, etc.). While everyone is told that they may be filmed, no one is told that in a few days they'll be receiving a video of their flight and dive experience – replete with Bible verses and an overlay of a prayer recorded by Henry. Best of all, each video is FREE OF CHARGE and they are NEVER displayed on any Internet medium unless the person receiving them does so of their own accord.

Henry and Marianna have mailed just over 1000 DVD's to participants in the past year and, as a result, have had around three dozen people contact them to say that either:

- They recommitted their lives to the Lord after watching the video.
or…
- They asked Jesus to be their Lord and Savior after watching the video.

One word of encouragement as you consider flinging seed is: Don't be discouraged if the first couple (or first dozen) you things try don't seem to produce any fruit. The reason is simple: Your primary job is to 'fling seed,' not to 'harvest the seed you've flung.' Believe it or not, the fruit of the harvest you'll eventually see probably won't have begun from the seeds you've flung personally. Rather, those who give their lives to Jesus on your watch will probably have had seed planted by someone else. Remember what the Bible states in 1 Corinthians 3:5-9:

"What, after all, is Apollos? And what is Paul? Only servants, through whom you came to believe – as the Lord has assigned to each his task. I planted the seed, Apollos watered it, but God made it grow. So neither he who plants nor he who waters is anything, but only God, who makes things grow. The man who plants and the man who waters have one purpose, and each will be rewarded according to his own labor. For we are God's fellow workers; you are God's field, God's building."

In other words, regardless of how much seed you fling and how hard you work at watering the seeds of the Gospel, it is up to God to bring it to fruition. Still, as we work to fling seeds and water those seeds that have already been flung, God will reward us for our work as long as we do it with His glory in mind.

The next time you want to 'fling seed,' remember that our Lord can give you all sorts of creative ways to do it. For more ideas visit the following sites:

http://www.crosswalk.com/who-is-jesus/evangelism

http://www.christian.org/answers/evangelism

http://www.simplysharejesus.com

Chapter 19

Practical Steps For Effective Outreaches

Forget politics and even personal convictions. The ONLY way our world is going to 'get better' is when Christians begin living out their belief in Jesus Christ.

Mahatma Ghandi may have hit the proverbial nail on the head when he commented: *"I like your Christ, I do not like your Christians. Your Christians are so unlike your Christ."*

One of the first things that any volunteer with 99 for 1 Ministries hears me say is:

"If the reason you don't give (monetarily, time, possessions, etc.) is because you're afraid someone is going to take advantage of you, allow me to set your mind at ease. **You WILL be taken advantage of. Period.** *Now that we've got this out of the way, let's get busy sharing Jesus' love with other people using Him as our*

example."

The point of my giving this of advice to everyone is because it's not a matter IF you'll be taken advantage of but, rather, WHEN. Before you're offended by anyone taking advantage of you remember that Jesus is 'the most taken advantage of person' who has ever lived. To paraphrase John 15:18, 'If people take advantage of you, keep in mind they took advantage of me first.'

Just as Jesus didn't allow Himself to be treated like a doormat, as you participate in outreaches you'll become better able to discern who is and who isn't trying to 'play both sides of the field' (i.e., those who are using you and others).

But, in order to develop this type of discernment you must be committed to long-term, intensive outreach into the lives of others.

While soft touch outreaches (handing out tracts, gas buy downs, coffee giveaways) have their place, true evangelism requires you to actually give of yourself and enter into the lives of others. Doing so will help develop spiritual muscles you probably never knew existed. Along the way you'll grow wiser and learn to differentiate between those who want to use you and those who truly want help.

A friend of mine, Jorge (pronounced George), told me of a time he was a missionary to an inner city neighborhood that illustrates my point about consistency.

"While serving in the mission field of Phoenix, Arizona in 1992, I desperately tried to get the youth of that area to lean on my friendship and see Jesus in my life. I was working with a mission that passed out food and clothing so I had many opportunities to mix with young people.

One day I was trying to get Israel, a seven-year-old, to open up to me. He told me, in no uncertain terms, he thought I would be like all of the other 'missionaries' that had come in the area to help. He suspected I would be there for a short time and then I'd go back home to live my life. It occurred to me that Christians had not invested long-term caring or discipleship in the lives they were touching.

I had the fortune of seeing Israel and being able to pour part of myself into him every day for nearly six months – at which time my father died and I had to go back to Alabama to close his business – and I lost touch with the little guy.

Around 10 years later I visited Phoenix again and tried to reconnect with the majority of the kids I'd met. Regrettably, <u>all of them</u> had succumbed to the pressures of a poor neighborhood (i.e., drugs, jail and teenage pregnancy). It broke my heart.

The bottom line is... consistency makes a difference. Had I been able to or had another Christian been willing to stay in the area and continue to pour the love of Jesus into the community I'm certain the outcome for these kids would have been different."

Reality Check:

The point of my sharing Jorge's story is that while some ministries begin based on the solid principles of outreach they often, relatively quickly, abandon all but the most shallow attempts to keep up appearances of holding fast to living Jesus out loud.

I personally know a pastor who preaches a great deal about outreaches but, in practice, he's abandoned them. He now writes about his experiences and even gives advice about going into the community to show the love of Christ but he doesn't do so himself any longer (or to any great degree). To me this smacks of the adage: 'those who CAN, DO' while 'those who CAN'T, TEACH.'

The reason ministries stop being effective in the outreach programs is because true outreaches are intense timewise, emotionally and spiritually. Still, regardless of why they stopped doing effective outreaches the point is that they've stopped.

I've conducted and read informal polls that asked (paraphrased): *"Why is it that your church doesn't do more evangelism projects?"*

The four most often stated answers to this question were:

1)	Lack of funds.
2)	Lack of participation.
3)	Lack of consistency.
4)	Evangelism is passé.

Of the four reasons given, the last three (lack of participation and consistency and the belief that evangelism is out of date or out of touch with today's society) are the biggest obstacles to effective outreaches.

They are also the easiest to correct.

Funding Outreaches

I don't spend a lot of time explaining how to generate funds for outreaches because, most often, the money to do whatever it is God wants you to do (show people He loves them by being His hands and feet) 'takes care of itself.' This is not to say that money will simply 'appear' out of thin air but that God will supply you the needed funds. How He chooses to do this is up to Him.

Letting those you know in on what you want to accomplish and praying God will touch their hearts or the hearts of those they know can bring about astounding results.

To be certain, money definitely helps with certain outreaches but others can be free or nearly free to set-up, bring to fruition and maintain. Examples:

•	Raking or Mowing Lawns
•	Parking Lot Shopping Cart Round-ups
•	Babysitting at Your Church for a Parent's Night Out
•	$1 Car Wash
•	Literacy Programs

- Diet or Cooking Classes
- Cupcakes to Your Neighbors
- And Lots More…

These types of outreaches are economical because they rely on help that probably already exists in your church or organization. Teens and children are two primary resources for those events that take a lot of energy (raking lawns, car washes) and adults can be instrumental in helping everything.

If you aren't very organized, find someone who is and ask them to help you in categorizing LOTS of ideas and then present them – one-on-one – to everyone you know who is a Christian. Don't be stingy – allow any and everyone who is a Christian (even if they aren't from your church or denomination) an opportunity to serve Christ by serving others with you. Remember: The more outreach teams you create, the more people can be positively impacted by God's gospel.

To me, the most important aspect of outreach isn't adequate monetary resources but, rather, adequate spiritual resources. Your heart needs to be focused on God and what He wants you to do for others rather than on what spiritual rewards you'll get. With this in mind, I suggest you learn to pray and pray a lot!

Tip: Think BIG when you're thinking FREE!

Increasing Participation

Participation in outreach programs is usually as simple as proper communication. I've found the most effective way of communicating is by taking to heart the maxim: 'Word of Mouth is the best form of advertisement.'

Undoubtedly, those who are most effective at increasing participation actually talk to people one-on-one. They call people on the phone, visit with others eye-to-eye or have a party to talk about plans – by the way, an 'Outreach Party' is MUCH better (and more fun) than a planning meeting. This doesn't mean that social media (Facebook, Handbook, BellyBook, MySpace, YourSpace, TheirSpace) or other ways of communication that lack a truly personal touch (email, voicemail) can't be used as an effective back-up. But, as a means of conveying the importance of something, nothing beats PERSONAL interaction.

Finally, the person in charge of 'getting the news out' must be excited about what is about to happen (i.e., ministering to those God loves). Excitement, even more than being able to deliver a cohesive, purpose-oriented message is the MOST important aspect I've been able to identify for increasing participation. If you don't believe me, think back to the last few years of political rallies. Many people who attend these rallies do so because they are 'caught up in the excitement' rather than being 'won over by the politician.' Of course, in the case of outreaches, we want people to not only be won over by the excitement but the reason for the excitement as well.

Managing Consistency

It's extremely important to be consistent in your efforts – not only for the sake of those you are reaching out to but for those who want to reach out with you.

Imagine how frustrated you'd get if you had an alarm clock that went off 'whenever.' Actually, I don't have to imagine the frustration because I've lived it. My son, at a young age, was playing with a battery operated digital alarm clock and accidentally dropped it in our toilet (don't ask me how, I have no idea). He retrieved it, poured the water out, set it in a corner for a few weeks, put in new batteries and turned it on – all without telling anyone.

The clock part of the machine ended up working absolutely fine but the alarm part of it didn't.

Over the next couple of weeks the alarm would go off at all hours of the day and night (3am, 2pm, 5pm, 4am, midnight, noon, you name it).

When the alarm would sound in the early morning, since I'm a fairly light sleeper, I'd jump up as if someone were breaking into our home. I'd run (or stumble) into his room, muttering under my breath things that disparaged our son's ability to set the doggone alarm properly – never realizing it had been damaged by water – and shut it off. A fortnight of answering the alarm's schizophrenic calls later, I threw the thing away.

The same type of frustration can develop when an outreach leader doesn't regularly schedule outreach events but, instead, plays it by ear. Being ready and willing to do things on the fly is part of life. But, consistency is needed because, even though people will want to participate with you, they need times to plan their lives around particular events.

Evangelism Is Still Important

In today's fast paced, extremely hectic, information-packed world many Christians consider evangelism to be outdated. Fewer things could be further from the truth.

While the notion of evangelism may be old and while there are certainly methods of evangelization we, as a society, may have outgrown, the reason behind evangelizing is as relevant today as it has been since Adam and Eve first began having children. Unless a person is told of Christ, shown Christ, introduced to Christ and becomes a Christian he or she will spend eternity without Christ (i.e., in Hell). So, if you're a Christian who believes that evangelism is outdated answer me this:

How were you introduced to Christ before you gave your life to Him?

Whatever your answer is, THAT is how you were evangelized!

Chapter 20

Muslim Man Comes to Jesus!

It doesn't matter who you are, where you're at, what you've done in the past, why you *feel* the *need* of a relationship with Jesus *now* instead of a year ago... rather it matters that when you are *ready* for a relationship with God you're able to find someone who can communicate with you (listen and respond) and introduce you to Christ.

To be a part of this introduction you must be dedicated to reaching people with the message of the Gospel keeping in mind you're looking something to build a bridge between pre-Christians and God.

Every relationship begins with and is built stronger by communication.

A story I hope will bring this advice alive for you occurred some time ago.

If you know much about me you know I suffer from a medical condition called xerostomia – a technical word meanig 'severe dry mouth.' Due to the radiation and chemotherapy I underwent when being treated for cancer I've been left with very few active salivary glands. In other words, my mouth doesn't produce spit. As such, I always chew gum and have a bottle of water, tea or a soft drink available. This is especially true at night because I wake up anywhere from ten to twenty times a night and take a sip from a bottle of water beside my bed because my mouth and throat are so dry the pain rouses me from slumber.

[As an aside, I had been taught that the story of the rich man and Lazarus (Luke 16:19-31), was a hyperbolic (exaggerated) parable for the sake of making a point. Even before I developed xerostomia I realized that every parable told by Jesus, even if it wasn't based in historical fact, provided a glimpse into a more important spiritual reality. Even so, I'd always been suspicious of the Luke 16-19-31 because it says the rich man cried out *"Father Abraham, have pity on me and send Lazarus to dip the tip of his finger in water and cool my tongue, because I am in agony in this fire."*

I was suspicious as to whether verse could be considered historical fact because I doubted a man who was in agony because of fire would beg for a simple drop of water from the tip of a man's finger to ease his pain. It made no sense to me. How could a simple drop of water provide any relief at all from the burning agony of hellfire? I wondered this until I'd put my body through a test. I decided to engage someone in a regular conversation without any water or gum in my mouth. I wanted to see what would happen once the saliva in my mouth dried up to the point I needed some amount of liquid in order to keep talking.

Here's what happened:

The first five minutes I was okay but then my mouth started getting pasty. Five minutes later I couldn't talk at all because my mouth and tongue were so dry it was getting painful. A few minutes later, I was drawing breath through my mouth and nose and struggling to keep my composure. I was in agony. I wanted to take a glass of water and gulp it down as fast as possible. Instead, I stuck the tip of my finger into the water and placed a single drop on the tip of my tongue.

I simply can't explain the relief I felt. It was as though I'd been working outside in the heat all day and had suddenly stepped into a cool, air conditioned building. After I'd confirmed a single drop of water was enough to provide some relief I drank the entire glass of water.]

This brings me to my story…

One of the commandments we've received from God is to always be ready to give an answer for the hope we have (1 Peter 3:15-17). At times I've completely missed my chance to witness to someone because I was in a hurry or simply too preoccupied with other things to recognize the opportunity God had put in front of me.

Not too long ago I was given the opportunity to witness to someone whose faith was diametrically opposed to those who hold a Christian worldview. Those of you who are careful readers will have noted I used a 'past tense' verb 'was' rather than 'is'. If you caught this, I'm certain you can guess how the story ends. But, for the sake of illustrating how powerful a personal testimony can be, I want to relate to you what happened.

I left my home early in the morning to start visiting hospitals. As happens most every day of my life, I simply get up and put on whatever is convenient. It was the same that morning. But, the twist is the shirt I'd put on – a black t-shirt that bore the image of two Band-Aids® in the shape of a cross and emblazoned with two words just above the Band-Aid: "Jesus Heals."

Uncharacteristically, I'd forgotten to bring anything to drink or gum to chew. I didn't notice my oversight until I was several miles away from home. By the time I'd realized my mistake I'd stopped singing along with the songs on the radio and was purposely holding my mouth closed and had begun breathing solely through my nose (which was still making the back of my throat ache).

I came to store, quickly pulled into the parking lot, entered the building, went to the cooler, got a bottle of water, opened it and took a refreshing drink. I grabbed another bottle and started towards the cashier. I approached the cash register, began looking through my wallet for the money need to purchase the water and never once did I look up at the person behind the counter… until he spoke.

"*So,*" the man behind the counter began. "*Jesus heals, huh?*"

"*Yes, He does,*" I said very enthusiastically. "*A friend of mine was in the end-stages of Parkinson's disease but Jesus healed him. I've had four friends of mine who were clinically diagnosed with Hepatitis C and none of them have Hep C any longer – in fact, one of them was told that he doesn't even have any bio-markers of Hep C in his system. That's pretty much impossible because a bio-marker would mean that you'd at least come in contact with Hep C before and yet this man, who had been checked and double-checked for Hep C and was going to have to undergo treatment for the same, no longer has any suggestion in his body that he was ever effected by it. And, I know several people, myself included, who had cancer – including stage four brain cancer – who are no longer afflicted by it.*

Why? Is there something going on that I can pray for you about?"

By this time I was looking directly at the cashier (a tall, thick young man whose heritage was most certainly middle-eastern). His mouth had kind of dropped open a bit but he quickly regained his composure and stated, rather forcefully. "*No, I'm Muslim.*"

Without thinking I said the first thing that came into my mind, "*Oh that's okay. Jesus doesn't mind. He knows you can change.*"

To say that I was shocked at what I'd just said wouldn't do how I felt justice. If I'd even thought about how rude (not to mention potentially inflammatory or dangerous) what I'd said might have sounded I wouldn't have said it. The rest of the transaction took place in relative silence with the exception of my saying 'Thank You' as I gathered my water and left.

As I climbed into my truck and put the keys into the ignition, I saw one of my books 'Death, Heaven and Back' on the passenger seat. It was the last of the case of books I'd purchased a week or so earlier to give to those I met and it just so happened I'd not found anyone during the last several days whom I felt led to give it to.

I remember thinking to myself: 'Wow. Wouldn't it be a shame not to use this as an opportunity to be a witness for Jesus?'

I prayed a quick prayer that God would allow my testimony testify of His grace and mercy and that the young man would be moved to accept Jesus as his Savior, grabbed the book and a pen, got back out of the truck, went back into the store, and, as I approached the young man I asked, "*What's your name?*"

He replied, "*Mohammed*," and I asked if it was spelled traditionally to which he nodded in the affirmative. As I inscribed a message inside the book for Mohammed a couple of other customers were rang up and left the store. I finished the inscription and noticed we were alone.

I turned the book over, took off the hat I was wearing, pointed to the picture and said, "*This is me and this is my story. I hope you'll call me if you have any questions once you've read it.*"

I handed the book to Mohammed, talked to him for a few more minutes – just so he would know I wasn't some rude Christian – and left on what I hoped was a good note. As you're about to read, I'm really happy I didn't miss the opportunity to speak to the young pre-Christian that day.

Several months after my 'chance' encounter with Mohammed I received an email from him. I'd like to share an excerpt from this letter I believe shows the power of being a witness for God. Mohammed wrote:

"Pastor Lonnie, I write this with tears in my eyes but joy in my heart. I doubt you even remember me. Several months ago you walked into a local store I used to work at. You were wearing a shirt that said "Jesus Heals" and it had a cross on the front of it. I remember that I said something dismissive but you smiled at me and said, "*Why, yes, He does. Is there anything I can pray for you about?*" When I told you I was a Muslim you said something like "*That's okay, you can change. Jesus won't mind.*"

I couldn't believe your audacity. I was highly offended but for some reason I did not get angry at you. When you left the store I was relieved because I thought you were some sort of crazy man because you had just told me that you had had cancer and that you had died and that Jesus allowed you to come back. I will remember forever when you walked back into the store. You asked me how to spell my name and then you signed a copy of your book and left it for me to read. I remember looking down at you and thinking to myself, *"This is a stupid Christian."*

I threw the book to the side of the counter and had intended to throw it away at the end of my shift. Almost a month later I was working the night shift, went into our cooler to stock it and found your book lying on top of some cases of beer. I picked it up and saw that someone had turned down the edges of a few pages and I looked at those first. Seeing your pictures of what you went through when you had cancer made me squirm. But I saw that in almost all of them you were smiling and this made me want to read more.

To make a long story short I read and re-read your book over the next 6 months. I called your number a few times but I hung up every time you answered and never left you a message (sorry). I began to ask myself if the things I had been taught about Jesus were true. Based on what you had written in your book I did not think they could be.

I started asking my uncle (who owns the store I used to work at) about my questions and he got really mad at me. Anyway, I could not stop thinking about some of the things you had written about so I went to a library and started reading the Bible. I could not believe what I read. It was so different than what I had been taught about the Bible and very, very different as to what I'd been taught about Jesus in Islam and what I thought Christians believed about Him.

One night, while I was at the store, I was all alone and I was supposed to be going to my uncle's house after work. I never went because a lady came in wearing the SAME shirt as you wore that one day. I asked if she knew you but she said she didn't. I asked her where it was she went to church and she told me and invited me to come after I got off that evening. She said her brother worked at a sandwich store just around the corner from where I did and that he would be happy to lead me to their church. I was not sure why I did it but I said Ok.

Honestly, by the time my shift was over I'd changed my mind. There was no way I was going to go to a Christian church. No way. But, God had other plans. Almost as if her brother (Tim) had been waiting to see me clock out, he walked into the store just as I was gathering my books up to leave. He walked up to me, confirmed that I was Mohammed, and told me his sister had invited me to their church and that he wanted to extend the same invitation. He was so kind and smiling and, for whatever reason, I heard myself say that I'd follow him to their church.

About half an hour later I found myself in a church filled with Jewish and non-Jewish Christians. I was sweating terribly out of fear or something. Anyway, the lady (her name is Cathy) came to me with another man and they both hugged me. I remember that when they did I was as still as a stone. The man was wearing traditional Jewish dress so when he hugged me I didn't know what to make of it – hugging a Jew is something I would have never, ever have done on my own. And, when Cathy hugged me I felt myself getting a bit light-headed. You see, it's not appropriate for a woman who isn't family to hug a Muslim man – especially in public. I thought for certain that Allah was going to strike me dead at any moment.

After meeting several other people (most of whom hugged me as if they'd known me forever), Tim showed me to a seat and told me that they were going to begin singing praises to God in a few minutes. I'd never, ever imagined that people could be so free in worshipping God. After a Rabbi had said a prayer and thanked everyone for coming the entire congregation was led in singing songs, most of them directed to Yeshua (Jesus in English. I'd grown-up calling Him Isa), for nearly an hour. To be completely honest, for the first half hour I was very tense but, after my initial shock (and seeing that no one was really watching what I was doing but seemed intent on worshipping) I relaxed a bit.

Once the singing was over the Rabbi led everyone in several prayers, announcements were made and, finally a message was delivered). Amazingly, I didn't feel much apprehension at all during the message because, while I thought it would be laced with comments against Muslims, the Rabbi spoke about how we should treat others – even those who hate us – and how God doesn't grade our righteousness on a curve but, rather, on whether or not we've accepted the sacrifice His Son Yeshua made for all of us.

To make my story shorter, I'll tell you that after the service was over the same Jewish man (John) who had hugged me when I first came into the church approached me. Again he hugged me. All this hugging from both men and women (mostly from women) has really taken a lot for me to get used to. Then, Pastor Lonnie, he did something I didn't expect at all. He directly asked me *"If you died tonight would you want to know for certain that you would go to Heaven?"*

I felt as if my face were on fire. I was both angry at the man for being so blunt as to suggest that he might be able to assure me that I'd go to Heaven when I died and I was confused as to why I felt as though he really did know something I didn't.

After what seemed like an hour of not saying anything out loud but talking silently to myself, I finally broke down in tears and said, *"Yes, I'd like to know how to be certain that I'll go to Heaven."*

I'll never forget what happened next. John gently wrapped his hand around the back of my neck and pulled me close to him. It was as if my father were embracing me. He just held me for a couple of minutes while I sobbed. Then, in the midst of my crying I felt other hands begin to touch my shoulders, my back, my head and arms and I listened as John led me in a prayer in which I confessed my sins, told Jesus that I loved Him and that I believed that He had truly lived for me, died for me on a cross and that He had been raised from the dead to show that He had power over death and life. I asked that His Father and the Holy Spirit to teach me what I didn't know and I cried out for His mercy. I told Him how sorry I was that I'd followed a false god all my life and that

I wanted nothing more than to follow the true and living God from now on.

Pastor Lonnie, I cannot tell you how free I felt after I prayed. I felt like I had been living with a vice on my chest and that all of a sudden it was gone.

My life has been hard since that night. I told my uncle about my decision to accept Jesus and reject allah the next day and he fired me and called my family and told them. I haven't been able to get any of them to speak to me because they know I do not believe in allah any more. Thank you for giving me your book and for dying. Please call me. I would love for you to meet my new Jesus family."

As an end note to Mohammad's story: Once he was fired by his uncle, Mohammed didn't have any idea as to how he was going to pay for college. He was within two semesters of having a Bachelor's degree in Engineering. A few weeks later, a man who attends the same church Mohammed was initially invited to found out about his plight. As it turned out the man owns an engineering firm close to Birminham and he agreed to pay for the rest of Mohammed's classes, books and room and board at a local apartment, if he would come to work for him after his degree was completed. Needless to say, Mohammed agreed and, today, he's gainfully employed, attending a Messianic Jewish Church and is going back to school to earn a secondary degree in Youth Leadership.

Chapter 21

What Being Salt and Light Is NOT About!

As I talked to Cheryl I came to realize that she really didn't know how Christians were supposed to act. She'd been raised by a domineering mother and a very subservient father, both of whom claimed to be Christians but neither of whom were good examples of being Christ-like.

As such, Cheryl was often very abrasive to those with whom she talked to about Jesus – to the point that they became irritated at the manner in which she spoke to them and they'd withdraw almost completely.

I'd seen it happen so often that I'd developed a mental picture of a snail that, while searching and sliming about, it's eye-stalks fully extended, suddenly runs into something unexpected and quickly retreats almost entirely into its shell – unwilling to reemerge until it's quite certain that whatever danger (real or imagined) might have been present has gone.

On a warm spring day Cheryl, along with a dozen others (including me), headed into the 'highways and hedges' to find people who were in need of jackets, blankets or food. It was decided that three people would form a team (partially so that we could take turns carrying the items we'd brought and partially for safety issues). I was partnered with Cheryl and Cindy and, though I didn't know it at the time, our outing would be a life-changing event for Cheryl.

Cheryl stood in stark contrast to Cindy, not only in physical stature but also in personality. Whereas Cheryl was tall and thin, Cindy was short and chubby. Cheryl had a 'I've gotta win at any cost' attitude about her almost all the time whereas Cindy seemed much more laid back and sensitive to the needs of others. More importantly, while Cheryl seemed to be a coiled snake, ready to strike at any moment, Cindy was more like a puppy... playful and approachable. As for me, I'd like to think that I'm somewhere in-between these two extremes but, truthfully, I tend to be more like Cindy than Cheryl unless I'm riled. Thinking back, I can definitely see that the three of us were one of the more balanced teams in terms of having two people whose attitudes were polar opposites of the other and one who knew how the others felt.

As a team-leader I was given the task of deciding where we should begin our quest to find those in need. I chose a modestly wooded area just behind a set of train tracks that set beneath an overpass (conveniently out of the line of sight of motorists but equally convenient to the roadways where many of the homeless panhandled when it wasn't either rainy or too cold).

[Note: Those who panhandle have learned, through trial and error, that even people who have a tender heart and are willing to share whatever they may have also have a tendency not to want to roll down a window and brave getting their clothes or the inside of their car wet and that cold air is a much greater deterrent (for whatever reason) than hot air. I mention this so that we, as Christians, won't be dissuaded by the same.]

Had it not been for the bug spray we'd covered ourselves in before entering into the woods we'd have been dined on by the many mosquitoes and other flying insects that, nevertheless, hovered around our faces. As it were, we soon found ourselves on a well-worn path that led us into a small campsite of sorts. It seemed to be less of a campsite than it was a hodge-podge of mats strewn across the ground (a few of which were covered by blue and silver tarps hung off the ground in an effort to deflect rain), tents (only a couple of which were in any type of decent condition and a few makeshift tables randomly placed here and there – most of which were covered with cans that held empty beer bottles or leftover foodstuffs.

As we entered the camp we were greeted by a few hoots and hollers as several of the men and women who live in what is called 'Tent City' recognized me. Soon we were hugging and laughing and talking to people with whom we'd never meet or socialize in the regular world – it wasn't that we would avoid them but, instead, they probably wouldn't feel comfortable enough in our world to come up to us and say 'Hi' unless we did so first.

I took the initiative and began handing out the items we'd brought with us. Cindy and Cheryl took the hint and began doing the same. Soon enough the ladies had broken away from me and were talking to two separate groups. As I talked to a couple of the guys I'd become very acquainted with over the past several months I also kept a watchful eyes on Cheryl and Cindy – less for the sake of safety and more to see how they acted and reacted towards those to whom we were ministering.

I sat down with Carl (a gentleman who'd once been a pipe-fitter with an oil company but whose life began to go downhill after he and his wife divorced and he'd tried cocaine). He wanted me to pray with him about a new job he was seeking. After we prayed he wandered off to find someone he wanted me to meet. Once Carl had gone I had the opportunity to watch how Cindy and Cheryl ministered to the small groups of people that had gathered around them.

Cindy was smiling, talking, hugging and asking those in her group how they were doing and what kind of things they really needed to help them better tolerate the environment in which they lived. Not only did she ask questions, she actually took notes about what she was told. After a few minutes Cindy was asked by a lady, whose nickname I found out was Cricket, the most commonly asked question I've heard during the course of ministering to people: "*Why are you doing this for us?*" Cindy smiled a big, wide, toothy smile and said, "*Because Jesus would do this if He were here on earth today!*" Then, unprompted, Cindy grabbed Cricket and gave her a gentle hug that, for a second or two, startled the lady. But, instead of reeling back from the hug, Cricket seemed to melt into Cindy's arms.

Two women who'd never met before exchanged an embrace that I've rarely seen between even the best of friends. When the hug ended I noted that both of the ladies had tears in their eyes. Later, Cindy told me that she felt a '*God-connection*' between she and Cricket and, sure enough, the two have become very good friends during the past two years.

Cheryl's group wasn't so lighthearted. She had quickly given out the items she'd brought to those who had followed her but, instead of smiling and hugging and talking to those she'd just met, she was preaching at them (not 'to' them but 'at' them – there's a *big* difference). For awhile those at whom she was preaching stayed around but that didn't last long. Cheryl began to question them about their relationship with Jesus, asking if they were certain that if they were to die that very night that they'd go to Heaven and warning them about the eternal torment of Hell. There was nothing wrong with her questions, but her delivery was extremely poor.

I'll remember until the day I die again how Bobby, a man with a skull tattoo around each eye, told Cheryl, "*I bet Jesus Hisself would be scared to talk to you girl!*" Even more clearly I'll remember that Cheryl reacted as though someone had slapped her. Cheryl's face screwed up in confusion as if she were trying to decipher what Bobby had just said and then, once she was certain he had insulted her, she took a half-step back. What she said next surprised even me.

"*Now look mister,*" Cheryl began and aimed her index finger at Bobby. "*I'm just trying to tell you the truth. If you don't accept Jesus Christ as your Savior you will <u>not</u> go to Heaven, you <u>will</u> go to Hell and you will <u>wish</u> that you'd listened to <u>me</u>!*"

Her emphasis on the words 'not,' 'will,' 'wish,' and 'me' were loud. Not just more audible than her other words but… LOUD!

Bobby wasn't putting up with her any longer and started walking away towards me. As he passed by he looked me in my eyes and muttered, *"You need to tell that woman there to have some manners."* With that he was gone.

I'll let you in on a little secret: You <u>never</u> want a scene like the one I just described to happen. Not only is it disruptive to the purposes of sharing Christ with others, it's also potentially dangerous.

Almost instantly I found myself in amongst Cheryl's small group and, thanks be to God, I was able to make everyone laugh. Soon I had invited everyone who wanted prayer to join us in a circle. We all held hands as we prayed but I noted several people had not joined us – namely, all those who had been talked 'at' by Cheryl. I made a mental note to come back later in the afternoon to assure everyone that we weren't angry with any of them.

Within a few short minutes (which seemed much longer), Cheryl, Cindy and I were headed out of the camp and back towards the main road. An hour or so later we were back at the church from which we'd left and I had a chance to talk to Cheryl. To her credit it was she who initiated our talk.

Before I began writing this section I contacted Cheryl to make certain that what I've written is correct – even though it is, to some degree, paraphrased.

Cheryl: *"Pastor Lonnie, I don't understand what I did to make everyone so angry at me."*

Lonnie: *"Why do you think that the people you met got angry with you and not Cindy?"*

Cheryl: *"I think it was because she wasn't standing up for Jesus like I was."*

Lonnie: *"Really? You really think that was the reason?"*

Cheryl: *"Well, maybe."*

Lonnie: *"The reason I ask is because I heard what Cindy was telling the people and I can assure you that she was telling people about the love that Jesus had for them."*

Cheryl: After being quiet for a long, long time she finally spoke, *"Maybe it was because I didn't show them Jesus' love but, instead, I talked to them about what would happen to them if they didn't accept Him. Is that right?"*

Lonnie: *"You tell me. Which approach would you rather have Jesus presented to you. The way you did or the way Cindy did?"*

Cheryl: Very sheepishly she said, *"I guess the way Cindy did. Maybe I was too aggressive or something?"*

Lonnie: My eyebrows went up into an arch, I smiled like a madman and asked, *"Maybe?"*

We both laughed and I continued, *"Cheryl, I think you've hit the nail on the head when it comes to the approaches you've described. Your approach is to present Jesus as a roaring taskmaster Who is set to devour His enemies whereas Cindy presents Him as a loving Shepherd. Believe me, I think that there are certain circumstances where your approach is just fine. But, by and large, I don't think it's as effective as the one taken by Cindy."*

Cheryl: *"But what about the passages in the Bible that say we're supposed to be 'salt and light' in this world? Salt purifies and the light dispels darkness, right?"*

Lonnie: *"Right. But, have you ever gotten salt in a cut? It burns and hurts like crazy doesn't it. What's the first thing you want to do when that happens? You want to wash the salt out of your wound as quickly as possible, right? Or, have you ever awoke to a bright light shining in your eyes? When that happens you want to close your eyes and hide your head to keep it from hurting, right? Well, that's the same thing I think happens to most people when they encounter Christians who approach them with Jesus as if He were their judge rather than their Savior."*

Cheryl: "*But He IS their Judge!*"

Lonnie: "*But, He is also their Savior – or at least He wants to be their Savior rather than their Judge. If you look in the Bible Jesus was very direct with people but He was also extremely kind. It was His kindness that made people flock to Him... not His sternness. There's no doubt that Jesus was an authority figure to everyone He met – even those who hated Him realized His authority – that's one of the reasons He was hated. Yet, it was very rare that He 'lorded' His authority over people. Instead, at least the way I read the Scriptures, He chose to show us how to lead others to Him by taking on the role of a servant.*

So, back to the analogy of being salt and light. Salt is a seasoning that is supposed to make food taste better and last longer and light is something that is supposed to dispel darkness so the path you are on is better able to be seen. In other words, they're supposed to be mostly pleasant. Certainly there are times when both can be used as a correctional tool but I think the Bible talks more about them being instruments of gentle persuasion. It's the same way with Jesus. He is shown to be the Almighty God and the most humble Servant, the Lion and the Lamb, our Father and our Brother, our King and our Friend. While Jesus is and will be the ultimate Judge of mankind, He preferred to live out His life among us in such a way as to bring us closer to Him – like a loving Father rather than as a stern Judge.

Cheryl, let me ask you a question: When you were first introduced to Jesus what was it about Him that made you want to accept Him as your Lord and Savior? Was it that you were scared that He was going to judge you and send you to Hell or was it that you felt His love for you?"

Cheryl: "*A little of both. I didn't want to go to Hell and I knew that if I didn't accept Jesus that that's where I'd go.*"

Lonnie: "*Okay, but, what made you believe that accepting Jesus would keep you out of Hell? What was it about Him that made you think He'd accept you – a sinner who deserved nothing but Hell –that He'd save you from eternal torment?*"

Suddenly, it was like a light went on in Cheryl's head.

Cheryl: *"What I read in the Bible about Hell terrified me but when I read about Jesus and how He treated others I knew that He loved them and, I guess, I thought He'd love me too."*

Lonnie: *"And do you still believe He loves you even though you've messed up pretty badly in the past couple of years – from what you've told me – or do you think His love is fickle and that He falls in and out of love with you based on what you do or don't do?"*

Cheryl: *"No, I believe that He loves me regardless of what I do because the Bible tells me that irrespective of what I do my righteousness is as filthy rags compared to His glory and that He will never, ever leave me."*

Lonnie: *"So, why do you think people got angry with you and not Cindy?"*

Cheryl: *"Because I was trying to scare people into loving Jesus while Cindy was showing His love to them."*

I hugged Cheryl and simply said, *"Yep."*

Conclusion:

Without a doubt, *trying* to scare people by showing them that Jesus won't tolerate even the simplest sin they've committed unless they accept Him as their Savior is MUCH easier than showing the love that Jesus has for them. But, scaring a person doesn't bring about true conversion whereas showing His love for them can. We're told over and over that not only does God love others but that we are to follow His example in loving others.

When Christ physically came to this world (as He will one day again), every act He performed (from having meals with sinners to casting demons into pigs) was done to show the love He had for people. Certainly, there were and are those who don't see His actions as loving but, regardless of their (hopefully temporary) blindness, it's true. For instance in John 3:16 He didn't say, "For God so hated sinners that He gave His only Son so that whoever will believe in Him won't burn in Hell forever." Instead, He used loving terms, terms of self-sacrifice, to show His love for us. What attracts people to Jesus is love, not fear!

Still, negative reinforcement is easier for most people to present when talking about Jesus. The reason is simple: Thinking back to our own childhoods which do we seem to automatically accept as being true – positive statements ('you're pretty, smart, nice,') or negative statements ('you're ugly, dumb, mean')?

If you're like most people you're much more likely to gravitate towards accepting negative statements that are made about you. Stand-up comics know this and they make us laugh when they do their skits about the way teens and adults 'cut each other down.' There are dozens of books available that show us how to 'put down' another person (Ex: *Giant Book of Put-Downs, Insults & Excuses!, The Best Book of Insults and Putdowns Ever, 1001 Insults, Put-Downs & Comebacks*, etc.). However, if you try and find just a few books (especially ones that are secular) about how to build-up the self-esteem of a person you'll find out the meaning of frustration.

Though painting a terrifying picture of an eternity in Hell is easy to do (even Jesus talked more about Hell than about Heaven), I think people who accept Him to escape the fury of Hell are likely to have done so as a 'get out of jail free card' instead of truly experiencing spiritual regeneration.

Truthfully, showing people the love of Jesus through your actions is difficult – especially for young Christians – because it goes against the nature you've lived with for so long.

However, if you're a Christian, it's important to remember that *you've got a new nature* and *you're no longer the person you were before you accepted Jesus*.

This new nature, given to you when you became adopted into the family of God, is empowered by the Holy Spirit – Who transforms you into someone who is holy and filled with life – rather than shackled to sin and death.

On a practical level this means that before you were a Christian you might have been able to _fake_ love for others but now, as a Christian, you can _truly_ love others the way Jesus loves them. The true power of the Gospel (as it's related in Romans 1:16), is that it transforms us (salvation) into something we weren't – His children!

While the law of God and His judgment against sin is just and righteous, we're told that God would rather love us (as His children) than judge us for rejecting Him (John 3:16-21). Remember: God tells us in James 2:15-17 (among others) that actions speak much louder than words!

Think about this:

If Jesus had come and proclaimed His love for us, long, loudly and fervently and yet He never demonstrated the same, would He have changed the world? No. Yet, when He decided to leave His throne, come here to live among us, healed multitudes and, finally died so that those who accept Him wouldn't owe a price for their sin (a price so steep there's no way any person could ever hope to pay it themselves), He proved He loved us. Then, when He raised Himself from the grave He further proved He had the power to break even the sting of death and proved to us what He had said all along was true: He was and is the King of Kings, the Lord of Lords and not even death or Hell has any hold on Him and, as His children, we don't have to fear anything at all.

I sincerely hope you'll take the more difficult road and begin to live out loud for Jesus so people are drawn to Him because of the love He wants to share with them rather than because they are fearful of Him as their final and ultimate Judge, Jury and Executioner. He most certainly is this but how He judges you will depend solely on whether or not you're in His family.

I can't help but believe, with every fiber of my being, that God would love EVERY PERSON ON EARTH to be His child based on the fact that He sent His Son to die so that 'whoever' (a word that is inclusive of all and exclusive of none) believes in Jesus (puts their entire faith in His Son's finished, atoning work) would have eternal life and that it is His desire that everyone would repent (from their sins and turn to Him for salvation) and would not perish (be eternally condemned to Hell). Of course, this doesn't mean, by any stretch of the imagination, that everyone will become His child. God is a realist and, as such, warns (repeatedly) of the impending doom each person faces without saving faith in His Son. Still, as long as the offer of salvation is 'on the table' (until a person draws their very last breath) it is our duty, as ambassadors of the Kingdom of God, to beg others on the behalf of Jesus to become reconciled to Him (2 Corinthians 5:20).

CHAPTER 22

Be a Witness for Christ Even When Things Aren't Going Well

Not long ago I was undergoing chemo and radiation treatments for Stage IV Oropharyngeal cancer and I had the chance to witness to both Janet and Greg. I wrote what you're about to read in an email I'd sent to those who were keeping up with my progress [*Death, Heaven and Back*, p. 180-191 and 207-216]. I tell you this not too brag about my evangelistic abilities (which are limited at best) but to encourage you that even when things are going badly we (as Christians) can and should be willing to be a witness for the love Christ has for everyone or, at the very least, to give it our best shot. I also mention the fact I was undergoing treatments for cancer so you'll better understand some of the references I make during the article.

Ministering to Janet – A Lady With Lung Cancer

Today I met Greg and Janet. The differences between the two couldn't have been more dramatic or similar. They were a study in contrasts and parallels.

Upon entering the Chemo Ward I found myself alone, with the exception of a few nurses who began flitting around me as if they were moths and I was a sugar-coated light in a dark alley.

I met Janet today. She was sitting in a chair in front of my own and was so full of fright that my eyes welled up with tears for her. This was her first day of Chemo and surgery is looming only a few weeks away. While her staging of cancer isn't as great as mine (II vs. IVa), the two tumors on her lungs need to be shrunk considerably before they can operate. The tumors, one each on the right and left main stem bronchus (the tubes that transition into your lungs from your trachea and allow you free-flowing oxygen), cause each breath to be constricted, thus reducing the overall circulation of blood-filled oxygen throughout her body. This restriction, in turn, has caused oxygen starvation throughout her system and is actually mimicking what might best be understood by most as organ-wide inflammation. The inflammatory response was so high in Janet that her M.D.'s initially believed that she had a combination of rheumatoid arthritis and rampant MODS (multiple organ dysfunction symptoms). She was in major pain. When she first arrived today she could barely walk. It wasn't until they started an I.V. with high levels of both Benadryl and Morphine that her pain subsided and she wanted to talk – and boy did she want to talk.

Her sister (Catherine) and her brother-in-law (Ben), both from out of state, hovered over her like a mother hen hovers over a chick. It looked very sweet. After they went back to the waiting room Janet told me she wished they'd quit hovering and then admitted that she needed them to hover. The situation was infuriating to her. She wanted her independence, was used to being independent and now knew she couldn't be independent and have any quality of life. Frustrating. I empathize.

The next words out of Janet's lips were these, "*I never thought this would happen to me. I can't believe how awful it is. I used to watch these shows on Lifetime where people were diagnosed with cancer and now I hate those shows. I can't believe I've got <u>cancer</u>.*"

While the words she spoke were interrupted by intermittent, tiny sobs and broken breaths one word and the emphasis she chose to put on that word came through loud and clear – *cancer*.

Imagine as if that single word were hissed through the lips of a serpent. Janet <u>feared</u> that word – *respected it* – and her body language said so. Even as it passed through her lips she averted her head as if she might accidentally see the word sort of slither away from her. When she turned back towards me tears had filled her eyes. Anyone could see she thought of cancer as a death knell too early in life.

Within seconds I had engaged her in conversation about the type of cancer that had invaded her body and what the protocol was for treating it. She had a fairly firm grip on what was to be expected and what the doctors were hoping would happen. She also seemed to have almost no hope in the words she repeated. It was like listening to my son recite for the umpteenth time our encouragement that if he gets a good education on the anatomy of bugs (or whatever) that his career opportunities might one day blossom so that he's no longer simply making 'chore money.' Janet, like my son, at that point, was more than happy with chore money (i.e., just getting along in life and being able to live).

I moved closer to Janet because we were both too tired to speak loudly across the room to one another. She seemed to appreciate my consideration. It was then I became bold.

"Janet, may I have permission to say something to you about the cancer in your body?" She hesitated but nodded her okay.

"Janet, don't be scared of cancer. I know that the word cancer is scary but it's just because most people hear or think about it in the most devastating terms. To me it's just another one of those 'things' that happen to a body for reasons we sometimes can't explain. The 'good' thing about cancer is that it isn't like the flu or a cold. You can't get it by just breathing germs from someone and it doesn't mutate as quickly as a virus. The bad thing is that people often don't find out they have cancer until it's all over their body – kind of like having the flu and waiting too long to go to the doctor to

be treated for it. But, in your case they know what type of cancer you have, they've told you they'll be able to operate, it's at a relatively low stage and the worst part is what you're going through now – I know it is for me. What I'm telling you Janet is that you shouldn't respect cancer any more than you respect a common cold. You've got to treat it differently but at least it can be treated. With a cold you just have to wait it out and hope your body can overcome the effects. With your type of cancer, you're not going to die from it."

I went off on a few rabbit trails during my discourse but she didn't seem to mind. At the end of my 'talk' her body was more relaxed and, for the first time in about ten minutes, she smiled. I took into consideration it could have been the drugs kicking in, but I also decided some of what I'd said had gotten through.

"What type of cancer do you have and how long have you been doing Chemo?" Janet asked me and nodded towards the three bags of solution hanging above my head.

"It's my second week. I go 5 days a week for radiation therapy on my head, neck, and chest in the room across the hall and I also come here for chemo. I've got what's called oropharyngeal cancer and I've been staged at IVa."

Her tired head shot up from her pillow, shock etched across her face. *"Stage four A? Isn't that bad?"*

I laughed and grinned like a fool (which made the etching on her face deepen a little. *"Well, it's not as bad as being dead or being audited by the IRS but, yeah, it's not real good."*

"What's going to happen to you?"

"Janet, I'm going to get through this. Just like you. I've already had a major surgery (I showed her my neck, she grimaced at the scar and my description of what the surgeons removed) and may have to have another one before it's all over with. Whatever it takes, it's just going to take. I've had other problems and will probably have more before I go home to be with the Lord. For right now, I'm pretty calm about this because He's here with me."

188

Snort!

The 'snort' was the first sound of life I'd heard from Greg (our older 'neighbor' in the Chemo Ward) and, as with most snorts of the caliber he gave, it didn't bode well. It was kind of a harbinger of doom snort. I'll get to his/our story later.

"*So, you're religious?*" Janet asked.

"*I'm a Christian. Some people call that religious, others call it a crutch, some call me a nut, but, yeah, I'm religious if by that you mean I've accepted Jesus as my personal Lord and Savior.*"

Agitated movement from Greg.

"*How about you Janet?*"

"*Well, I don't go to church or anything but I believe in Jesus. I just don't know why He'd let me get cancer?*"

"*I don't know why I got cancer either but I don't think Jesus gave it to me directly — He might have, but I don't think so. I just think we live in a fallen body, a body that's been hurt by sin, by the way we live and cancer is sometimes a result of living in a world that evil is allowed into. Since you brought up Jesus, would you mind telling me who you think Jesus is? What's He like? What does Jesus think of you — of Janet?*"

Talk about silence. Tick, tock, tick, tock, hmmmmm, tick, tock, tick, tock, hmmmmm, beep, beep, beep (the sounds of a wall clock, the hum of our dripping chemo, and alarms alerting the Chemo Nurses that a bag somewhere needed to be changed could be heard as I waited for her answer).

Finally...

"*I don't know how to answer those questions. Not really. I mean, Jesus, the Jesus of*

189

the Bible, if I remember, was a really nice guy. He never got angry, He never called anyone names, He never hurt anyone and He healed people. I guess. I mean, he died and rose on Sunday – that's why people go to church on Christmas and Easter. I don't really know what religion He was if that's what you mean?"

The look of disquiet on Janet's face was obvious. She was searching for answers she just didn't have.

Skirting the many obvious theological 'jump-in' points she'd offered me, I asked Janet how old she was and when she said 52 I was honestly taken aback. She looked much, much older than her chronological age (I found out why later but that's for her to tell you if you ever meet).

"Janet, do you mind if I tell you a little about the Jesus that I know?" She indicated it'd be okay and I quickly prayed that what I was going to say would minister to her. This was not a sermon I'd prepared.

"Janet, we read in the Bible that Jesus was not only a good man and a good teacher but that He Was and Is God. As you said, the reason we celebrate Christmas and Easter is because Jesus decided to come to Earth as a human, that's a fancy word called the Incarnation, and to live among the people He'd made – in other words humans – and then He rose from the dead, that's called resurrection. Did you know He was a pastor whose ministry only lasted about three years and after those short few years He was killed?"

She nodded hesitantly.

"Did you also know Jesus was almost 20 years younger than you when He willingly died a horrible death, a death more horrible than anything we could ever suffer from cancer a car wreck or even torture by the hands of other people? The reason it was so brutal and horrible is because Jesus wasn't dying for things He did – because He did absolutely nothing wrong, even the judge who sentenced Him to death admitted Jesus was sinless and that He was pure and innocent. What made Jesus' punishment and death so horrible is because when He died, while He was suffering, He asked God the Father to allow Him to be punished for every single, solitary, bad thing that you and I and everyone who has ever lived or will ever live will ever do. When we do things that aren't pleasant to God, that's called sin and it makes God very unhappy – sometimes

190

mad — but always sad. We're told that when Jesus died, He took to His grave ALL of the things that make God mad or sad at us and they were buried with Him. Janet, what happens to a pet, no matter how much you love it, if it dies and you bury it? Is it still around or is it gone?"

"It's gone. You can't get it back."

"Right. So, when the sins Jesus took with Him to His grave were buried they were gone — forever. Period. No coming back."

"But, what about when He came back from the dead?" Her eyes were piercing now, as if she were inspecting me for any amount of falsehood. *"Didn't they come back with Him when He got back alive again?"*

"Janet, that's a good question. Here's what happened. When Jesus, who is God the Son, died, His Father decided that every sin for which Jesus had died would be forever forgiven as long as the person who had or will commit them would accept His Son's payment for those sins. You see, sin is just like a debt. It's something we owe someone for. In this case, God initially made us perfect — starting with Adam and Eve. Since that time we've been really doing ourselves in by sinning in ways our original parents probably never even imagined. Each sin is like a red mark against our name and against God's name since He's the One who created us. So, the ONLY way to get those red marks removed was to have someone come up and pay our tab, so to speak. That person is Jesus. So, when Jesus died, it was like He said, cover Me in as much red as you need but let Me take on their debt. I'll pay it all. Once it's paid, I'll return and give them the chance to become the person We wanted them to be in the first place, only they won't have the weight of debt hanging over their heads. Janet, do you know what redemption is? Do you know what it means when you redeem a coupon at the store?"

"It means you trade something in for something new?"

"Right! And, what happens to that coupon you redeemed on something new? Can you use it again, or is it all used up?"

"It's all used up?"

191

"Right again. But, what does the store do to that coupon you just used for the new thing?"

"Oh, they tear it up so it can't be used again. I used to work at Sears and sometimes people would try to reclaim a used coupon but we couldn't let them do that because it had already been used by the original owner."

"Janet, that's what Jesus did for you and for me. When He died and was put into that grave He took with Him all the coupons of debt, of sin that you and I have or ever will accumulate and carried them to His Father. Even though it didn't happen like this, I like to imagine that Jesus carefully placed each and every coupon out on a huge, big ol' desk, each coupon bearing the name of a person with all their sins on it. Then, God the Father, looks down on all of those coupons, all of those certificates of debt, maybe Lonnie Honeycutt's being the most stained with red check marks, and says to His Son, Jesus. "Jesus, who is going to pay for Lonnie's debt to Us? It's a really big bill and there's no way he can ever pay for it himself." Then, Jesus smiles at His Dad and says something like, "If Lonnie will accept My payment for his debt and willingly turns his life over to Me so he can truly be free and live the life I've always wanted him to live, I want to redeem Lonnie's coupon. But, it's up to Lonnie. It's still Lonnie's decision. I want to do the same for Janet. That coupon has everything on it Janet has done or will ever do, that is offensive to Us. It's full of red. But, if she'll accept Me as the redeemer of her coupon, I'd like to pay the price that she'd otherwise have to pay."

The Father looks at His son like a judge looks at a familiar but known criminal – wanting to show mercy but also knowing justice has to be served and He asks, "What type of payment do you offer for Lonnie and Janet and all the rest of humanity."

Jesus steps back from His father and hold up Hands. A light shines on the young man's body and even though blood covers Him from head to toe, gashes hang with flesh from the torture He'd received a few hours ago – just before and while He was on the cross – and, even though He's been so hideously beaten, beaten so badly He doesn't really look human, Jesus smiles.

"I offer as payment the ONLY THING you and I can accept as payment. I offer a completely pure, sinless, debt-free life, given up for those who have sinned against Me, knowingly or not. I offer My life for theirs. I offer the life of the One who made them

in the beginning, Who sustains them even now, Who loves them eternally, and Who never had to face mortal death but who did so because I knew they could never repay the debt they owed to Me themselves. Since it is to Me they owe the debt, I ask that You accept My payment for them so those who will can live with Us forever and ever."

The Father smiles, agrees, raps a heavy gavel, grabs His Son and, together with the Holy Spirit, they rejoice that all the coupons have been redeemed. With that Jesus scoops them all up, hands them to the Holy Spirit and says,

"Okay, here's the plan. Before people are going to catch on to what just happened, I need to go back and visit with them a bit more. So, you take these redeemed coupons, keep that one for Lonnie handy, he's going to really be excited about it, let me get cleaned up and in a couple of days I'm going to go back to the ones I just left. After they see me I'll tell them to spread the word that I have power not only over life but of death too. Once they start telling everyone about what's just happened, You get ready to start redeeming those coupons each and every time anyone says 'Yes, I'll accept Your payment for me' and truly wants Us to help them change their lives. Of course, You and I both know that some people will 'just say the words' but We'll know so, if they just talk the talk, the coupon doesn't get redeemed until they really mean what they say. If they don't really accept My payment for them, if they're just agreeing as a kind of 'get out of jail free card,' their coupon will be given back to them at the time of their death, unredeemed. Also, once a coupon is redeemed I want You to throw it into the Sea of Forgetfulness so that no one, especially the devil, has any access to it again. That'll really irritate him. Got it? Good."

I gave Janet a couple of seconds to grasp what I'd said and then I continued, "Janet, three days later, on Sunday morning, Jesus brought His own body back to life, came back from the dead and do you know what He used to show He'd redeemed all of our debts? A redeemed body! I mean when He came out of His grave, the tomb He'd been laid in, His body was completely NEW. Even though it still bore the scars from His old body so that people would know who He was, everything else about it had been changed. Gravity, time, space, nothing had a hold on this newly redeemed body of His. He could still touch, taste, smell, hear, see and hug people but His body was perfect – it was never, ever again going to die or hurt or even get old.

Better yet, He went around and started telling people that the body they were seeing now, a body that used to be dead but was now alive, was one they could have, too. All *they had to do was accept the payment He'd already made for them.*

Of course, some people believed Him. Some didn't. Some do today. Some don't. But, here's the point, Janet: Jesus is NOT mad at Lonnie. He's NOT mad at Janet. Does this make any sense at all?"

Janet had closed her eyes and for long, long moments she was quiet – so long I thought she might have drifted into a restful sleep. Finally, Janet opened her eyes and just stared at me. Honestly, it was kind of eerie. I could see the drugs had been working on her because she looked a bit loopy.

"It makes sense. A little sense. But…" There was another very long silence, punctuated by tears welling up in her eyes and when I heard her voice again it was a bit raspier than before. *"I know the Bible says that Jesus, since He's God, can forgive sins before we believe in Him when we accept Him as God and Savior but… what about the things I've done after I tell Him I want him to be my Savior?"*

It was my turn to choke up a little – not just because I felt sympathy for Janet but also because I could empathize with her. I know what it's like to personally know, without a doubt, that I've let my Lord down even after telling Him I'm sorry and trying to do what would be acceptable in His sight.

"Janet, remember how we talked about the redemption of coupons?" She nodded. *"You said that when you worked at Sears sometimes a person would come back in and try to use the same coupon again, right?"* Another nod. *"Were they allowed to?"*

"No, because they'd already cashed it in and it was either torn up or marked through."

"Well," I smiled. *"You know what Jesus would tell us if we tried to use the same old coupon He'd already redeemed? He'd say, 'Nope, can't do that. I've already used the one with Janet's name on it. Lonnie's too. They're mine now and nobody else can ever have 'em. Since there's only one coupon per person, you don't have any left. You*

might want it back but you can't have it back. All the debt that was on the ticket has been wiped out. I paid for it all and I'm not putting any of it back on your account. If I did I'd have to die for you all over again and I'm NOT going to do that. So, sorry, you're out of luck. You're all mine. Besides, Janet, even if I wanted to get the coupon back I couldn't because I've already forgotten where it is – it was put at the bottom of the sea so it might as well be as far as the East is from the West as far as you're concerned.'"

"Does the Bible really say that?" She was staring at me again but this time there was less dopiness in her eyes and more desire for the truth.

"Yeah, it really does. I mean, it says it differently but it means the same thing." I gently took her hand. *"Janet, you don't have to be scared of God. He really does love you. You know what you've done that isn't right and so does He. But, He's willing to cancel out every bit of your debt, to erase every bit of sin from your soul because He's already paid for it. The best thing is that if you'll allow Him to do so, He'll adopt you and you'll actually become His daughter – an honest-to-goodness, real-life princess. Whaddya think?"*

"I'm really tired but could you tell my sister where to find that stuff in the Bible?"

"Sure."

"You really seem to believe what you're saying." She let my hand go and settled back into her neck pillow. *"You have a piece of Doritos on your moustache."*

With that Janet closed her eyes and we stopped talking. I almost laughed out loud at her parting comment. Sure enough, I'd been talking to her the whole time with a small piece of Doritos corn chip on my moustache. What a bonehead. Haha.

As an epilogue to my conversation with Janet I'd like to say that I don't know if anything I said actually penetrated but some of it seemed to. For those who are professional theologians, I apologize for using what you may think are base examples of the redemptive plan of salvation.

To all who are Christians I'd like to remind you of the exhortation we're given in Scripture: *"But in your hearts set apart Christ as Lord. Always be prepared to give an answer to everyone who asks you to give the reason for the hope that you have. But do this with gentleness and respect, keeping a clear conscience, so that those who speak maliciously against your good behavior in Christ may be ashamed of their slander. It is better, if it is God's will, to suffer for doing good than for doing evil. For Christ died for sins once for all, the righteous for the unrighteous, to bring you to God. He was put to death in the body but made alive by the Spirit, through whom also he went and preached to the spirits in prison who disobeyed long ago when God waited patiently in the days of Noah while the ark was being built. In it only a few people, eight in all, were saved through water, and this water symbolizes baptism that now saves you also – not the removal of dirt from the body but the pledge of a good conscience toward God. It saves you by the resurrection of Jesus Christ, who has gone into heaven and is at God's right hand – with angels, authorities and powers in submission to him."* 1 Peter 3:15-22 (NIV '84)

The first part of this verse says we're to set Jesus apart in our hearts as Lord. This means that He either IS or ISN'T our Lord. If He IS that sets us up for following His command to *"Always be prepared to give an answer to everyone who asks you to give the reason for the hope you have. But do this with gentleness and respect..."* This means whether we really feel like it or not – I definitely didn't 'feel' like chatting that day. But, even though I didn't feel like following His command, I can only imagine how much shame I'd feel had I not seized upon this opportunity when, at the Great White Throne Judgment, I'd have seen this lady confined to Hell for eternity.

The construction of this command in the original language is remarkably similar to commands we give our children in English when we tell them, *"Always be on your best behavior so people know what kind of parents you have."*

In other words, it's not a 'letter of the law' command. We aren't being told to wait until the moment someone specifically asks, *"What's the reason for the hope you have in Jesus?"* It's a general command to tell everyone we can about the hope Jesus gives us. It's synonymous with the Great Commission in which we're told to tell the Word of God to everyone who will listen. Just like manners shouldn't be used *only* when people ask us to use them, our witness to others is a continuous action.

In short, 1 Peter 3 tells us that 'Jesus died for all our sins ONE TIME – the Righteous (Jesus) was sacrificed for the unrighteous (Us) for the single-minded purpose of bringing us back to God.'

We're also told God is patient – before He destroyed the world with water He waited for nearly 1000 years for people to 'get the hint' (a pretty big hint) preaching, a huge boat being built out in the middle of nowhere, the threat of a downpour of rain (which had never been seen before) – but that His patience can be exhausted – after the Ark was built, judgment came.

Finally, we're told that we're saved by the resurrection of Jesus who holds ALL authority in His hands. All-in-all, this one passage gives us a pretty good glimpse into the condition we're all in before asking Christ to be our Savior, our condition after accepting (or not accepting) Jesus as Savior and some of what we have to look forward to because of our decision – life <u>with</u> or <u>without</u> Jesus FOREVER!

I encourage you… the next time you have the opportunity, step out on a limb and do as Jesus commands us to do, tell people about Him. Don't worry whether or not you're going to 'mess it up.' Just do what you know you're supposed to do and trust that He'll take care of the rest. I promise, He can!

Greg – The 81-Year-Old Atheist

You were introduced to Greg a few pages ago. He was the older gentleman who kept grunting as I talked to Janet (the new Chemo patient). In any case, after Janet had fallen asleep I began a conversation with Greg and found he was a very interesting fellow who had led a fascinating life.

One of the most interesting things Greg told me was that he'd been one of the first African American men placed aboard a fighting ship in the Navy. It was a destroyer but I couldn't make out the name when I listened to the recording of our conversation. He may have said it was

197

the Manley but that probably isn't correct. Anyway, he and I talked about this part of his life quite a bit and I found that he'd not only been in both WWI & WWII but also in the Korean War as a consultant of some type (he mumbled a bit and I didn't catch it).

The short version of his military history is as follows: Greg 'applied' with the Navy at the age of 16 because he was tired of working on a cotton farm. He didn't have a high school education, he was black and he was underage. To hear him tell the story, none of that really mattered.

The recruiting station he'd signed-up under was 'progressive' and wanted blacks in the military (he kept using the term 'blacks' so I'll use it liberally here). He didn't have a birth certificate to speak of but, then again, neither did the nineteen other young black teens who went with him to the station. Once accepted they were put to work below decks as cooks, janitors and the like. Their quarters were a distance from the 'white boys' and sometimes he just slept near his station so as to not get into trouble. Even though the Navy wasn't very accommodating to his needs as a minority, Greg figured that he'd be able to 'see the world' better from a ship than from a field in Alabama. And, apparently, he has.

Our conversation began once Janet fell asleep – since Greg used some rather vulgar words I've taken the liberty of softening them.

"So, you're one of them pastor guys, huh? Never found much use for priests myself. Did you hear about the preacher the other day what was caught with them young boys. He had all this money out on the bed and these fancy watches and told 'em, "y'all take whatever you want because you know what I want!"'

He waited for a response while I stared blankly at him. I couldn't believe what an upfront attack he was beginning.

"Well, it's pretty apparent that he's a poor excuse for a minister, isn't it?" I told him. *"I hope the cops got him and locked him away – not only for being a pervert but for impersonating a man of God."*

"So," he continued unabated. *"You get your jollies from coming in here an telling*

fairy tales to people like her? Don't you think it's a little unfair to take advantage of her since she's so sick and all? She's likely to believe anything just to have some hope."

"Greg, I figure we're on a level playing field here. I'm just as sick as she is. In fact, I'm much sicker. Now, between you and me, I don't know which one is worse off. You're old and getting feeble and I'm in a younger but just as feeble body, speaking immunity-wise. Besides, I don't consider them fairy tales. You did notice that I didn't once mention Peter Pan, Santa Claus, or Allah."

"You think Allah's a fairy tale?"

"Sure, don't you?"

"It's just, I thought all you religious fanatics said that Allah was just another name for 'Gooodddd.'" He let the last word roll out of his mouth as if he were a preacher with passion.

"Well, it is the name of 'a' god, just a false one. Allah isn't anything other than an idol — just like the gods worshipped by people who construct likenesses of their deities on totem poles."

"So, you think that lady needs a crutch, do you? Don't think she's strong enough to face up to her disease all by herself?"

I smiled. *"That's an interesting question coming from someone who is wearing glasses, two hearing aids and who is also being treated for cancer. What's wrong? Do you think you need that many crutches? Aren't you strong enough to face up to weak eyes and ears and a body that's infected?"*

Greg sat up straighter. *"Hey, these aren't crutches. I need these because there's something really wrong with my body. If I didn't have this stuff I wouldn't get through the danged day."*

"So, crutches, things that help you make it through the day, are okay, as long as there's something really wrong with you?"

"*Yes.*" He snorted and blew his nose. "*But the garbage you're feeding her isn't anything but poison. Talking about some fool who died for sins and who is supposedly god almighty and who brings peace to all the people of the world. All we've got to go on is what other people have said is true. That's just hogwash and you're a moron if you believe it.*" His accusations dripped with sarcasm.

"*Hmmm,*" I sat back in my recliner and looked long and hard at Greg, praying I'd know how to respond to what was an obviously hardened heart.

"*What's the matter? Did I hurt your sensibilities?*" He mocked and wiped something out of his nose.

"*Mine?*" I smiled. "*No, not at all. I mean seriously, you just called the God I love and adore, the God who has changed my life forever, the God over Heaven and Earth, over Life and Death, the One who is above all a 'fool' and you've told me that believing in Him is hogwash. Believe me, calling me a moron doesn't bother me one iota. I've been called a lot worse by people who know me a lot better than you.*"

We sat there in silence for a few minutes until I nodded to capture his attention away from the television playing quietly in the corner.

"*Greg, can I ask you a question or two?*"

"*Shoot.*"

"*What's your real beef with God? Why won't you even consider the possibility that He's real?*"

Without a seconds hesitation he said, "*Sickness for one. Evil for another. If God's supposed to be all-loving why would he allow either to exist.*"

"*But, how do you know He's supposed to be all-loving?*"

"*The Bible says so, doesn't it?*"

"*Ah, so can I assume, for the sake of argument, that we can limit our discussion to the God described in the Bible rather than the one in the Quran or the Book of Mormon?"*

"If that's the one you know best, sure, but they're all the same."

"Well," I shook my head, *"They're not all the same but I just wanted to wrap my mind around some kind of foundation. So, what about sickness bothers you?"*

"It just shouldn't happen. I haven't done anything in my life to deserve this. This makes you feel lousy. And, look at you, you're supposed to be some kind of 'man of god' and he won't even cure you."

"Who says He won't? He just may not have done it yet."

"That's just childish thinking. It's like someone saying, I'm really first even though I came in last because it's my attitude that determines my altitude. Something stupid like that. The fact is the person who comes in first is first and the person who comes in last is last. I'm sick, you're sick, everyone in here is sick of something – we're born dying. It's just not fair and it's not something a loving god would do if he had the power to control the health of those he created."

"That's a mouthful. Greg, do you have any kids?"

"Sure. A passel of them. Some I haven't even met. Reckon I got about half dozen children that I know of, three who live around here."

"When your children were growing up, maturing and they asked you to do something you had a reason for not doing would you go ahead and do it?"

"No."

"Even if they couldn't understand what your reasons were for not doing it?" My point was made and I saw it register on his face. He'd been backed into a corner, but he was agile.

"Well, yeah. But, we're talking about you being sick – with cancer. Why wouldn't God cure you – especially someone like you – of that?"

"Greg, first of all you don't know who 'I' am." I made a grandiose flourish with my arms – the I.V. tubes bounced to and fro as if they were the tentacles of some emaciated, stainless steel octopus. *"I could be like the preacher you hear about on the news who molests children or the truck driver who secretly hides bodies in the back of convenience stores, or the little, unassuming white guy who also happens to be the Grand Wizard of the KKK. But, thankfully, who 'I' am or who 'you' are doesn't really matter in this case. You're looking at sickness as if it's something terrible in and of itself rather than just being what it is. Besides, it's not like I'm going to die."*

"Heck, you might, you never know. Being a Christian doesn't give you immunity to death. Cancer could kill your butt just like mine." Greg gestured with a meaty finger as if to mark '1' on some unseen chalkboard in the air.

"That's where you're wrong, Greg. As a Christian, I am immune to death. Absolutely immune. I'll never die. Oh, this body I'm in might die but even it'll be redeemed, made alive and better one of these days. So, I don't have to fear death. Your butt, as an atheist, has one cheek in the fire and one in the frying pan so to speak. What's you're escape plan?"

Greg just looked at me. His face screwed-up in a fashion I couldn't really read. It could have been that he either thought I'd just crossed over the line and was about to lambaste me with a tirade on being nice to your elders or he was contemplating running from the Chemo Ward just in case I <u>was</u> a cancer-riddled uni-bomber. Or it could have been gas pains. Who knows. Whatever it was, the silence between us lasted a long, long time. Finally, I was prompted by the Holy Spirit to continue.

"Greg, you said you were stationed on a battleship. Did you ever see wartime action?"

"You mean did we ever kick the living poop out of people. Yeah."

"Greg, what's a depth charge like? What does it feel like when one of those go off?"

"Oh, man, it's something else." His eyes lit up and you could see him remembering the events he was about to unfold as if they had happened

just yesterday. *"You drop one of those babies and when it blows I don't care where you are in your ship, it feels like it's going to rip something apart. I used to almost poop myself every time one of these things went off and they went off a lot sometimes."*

"So, you used to drop them yourself?"

"Me? Heck no. I was mostly a cook during those days. I never actually saw any of 'em being dropped. I'd just hear the command and feel the shock."

"So, how do you know it was a depth charge they were dropping?"

"Oh, the guys above deck were in charge of that. The C.O. would give the 'go,' those boys'd swing into action and pretty soon – BOOM! Hot darn, that must have scared the stew out of anybody in a sub." Greg was swinging his arms to and fro, being a little too loud and coming precariously close to knocking over his own I.V. pump. It was fun to watch but I was glad I was on the other side of the room.

"I've never been in the military." I continued. *"What's the C.O.?"*

"That differed depending on the shift."

"I mean, in general."

"Oh, it's the Commanding Officer. He's the one who gives the orders to fire the guns and drop the charges. You either listen to him or you're in the brig. I learned that the hard way one day and it cost me a week."

"Were there any African Americans dropping the charges?"

"Blacks? No. Not when I was there. We was just cooks and janitors and cannon fodder. Unless things got really bad me and my boys kept our butts down, tight and out of sight. Once I went up on deck when we were in the thick of things and I puked all the way back down into my hole. It was like hell had come to Earth and Satan himself was throwing body parts at me. But, I got to see the world."

"Did you ever drop one yourself?"

"Me? No, boy, I'm black."

"I mean after blacks were accepted into the rank and file of the Navy."

"No, I never got that close to them."

"Then," I inquired. *"How did you know they were actually dropping depth charges and not just hand grenades?"*

Greg looked at me with a look that posed the silent question, 'does your Mama know how stupid you are?'

"Well, for one, they ain't no grenade in the world what could make an entire ship rattle like one of them charges. And, when we went back up on deck to help clean up or to disembark I was shown the depth charges and where they were packed and kept."

"Oh, so you actually saw a depth charge that had exploded?"

"No," Greg rolled his eyes at me. *"Those would be the ones at the bottom of the ocean."*

"Greg, what would it take for you to believe in Jesus as God?" The question caught him unprepared but he recovered nicely and seemed to appreciate the new question.

"That's easy. I'd believe if he would come down and speak to me face-to-face. If he'd show himself to me then I'd believe. Otherwise it's only so much hearsay and you can't count on hearsay."

"Ok, let me get this straight." I started using my fingers to count points. *"You never actually saw a depth charge go overboard and explode. You never saw a depth charge that had exploded so that it could be checked against one that hadn't. You were told where the depth charges were kept. You were told what depth charges were supposed to do. You were told what depth charges were supposed to do to subs. And you assumed that when your ship rocked it was because of one of these supposed*

depth charges. Further, you took the word of a superior officer and of the rank and file military men that what you knew about depth charges was correct. Did I miss anything?"

Greg hesitated. He could tell that something had just happened. *"Um, no. I don't think so. That's about right."*

"Greg, you might just be only 81-year-old idiot I know." That comment stopped every conversation in the room. Finally, he said, *"I've never had a Christian talk to me like that."*

"Well, maybe it's about time." I shook my head in astonishment. *"Do you realize how hard it is for a pastor to talk to people who are hypocrites?"*

"What? I ain't no hypocrite."

"Sure you are. It sounds like you have a double standard for Christ and just about everything else."

"What do you mean?" Greg was obviously angry and the blood pressure machine he was hooked up to showed a rise.

"Well, you tell me that all we have to go on when it comes to my faith in Jesus Christ is hearsay – what others say is true – and that we can't trust that type of hogwash. Then you tell me about an experience in the Navy and you admit that you've come to a conclusion based on the exact same 'hogwash' you don't want me accepting, namely, the testimony of other people about something you don't know anything about firsthand. That sounds pretty hypocritical."

Greg finally 'got' where I was going. *"That's not fair. What you're doing is trying to convince me that I should accept the same evidence for a supernatural being as I should for something natural."*

"No, no. That's not what I said, that's what YOU said. You said you'd believe if He came and talked to you and showed Himself to you. That's what I would call wanting the same evidence. But, I don't necessarily disagree with you. That's called plain evidence. Still, you didn't wait until you had 'plain evidence' before deciding that

depth charges were real."

"That's because I KNOW depth charges are real. I've felt them. I've heard them. I've..." he started.

"...Assumed that what you felt and heard and were told about were depth charges. That's all you've done."

"Well," he pointed a work worn finger at me. *"What kind of evidence do you have about God?"*

"I've seen Him work."

"Bull."

"Nope, not on bulls, on people. He does probably work on bulls but, as for what I've seen, He's worked on people. In the past 2 years I've seen two people completely cured of Hepatitis C, without going through any treatment protocol, mind you, and one man completely cured of Parkinson's disease. Plus, I know all three of these people personally. That's pretty strong testimony."

"It's no different than mine with the depth charges," he argued.

"Yes, it is. In at least one way."

"What?" His arms were folded.

"The guy who let you into the Navy at sixteen years old and assigned you to a battleship... did you know him very well?"

"No, he was just the guy at the recruiting station."

"How about your C.O.? Did he really care about you or were you just another number, a token to get a feather in his cap as long as none of the blacks under his care got hurt or killed?"

Greg hesitated. *"No. Those guys didn't care about me or my boys. All they cared about was numbers. That's all we was to them, just numbers."*

I gotta tell you folks, my heart went out to Greg at that moment. He'd just verbalized something he probably hadn't really wanted to think on in a long, long time. It showed on his face. I continued, much softer now.

"Greg, even though you knew those men didn't really care about you or your friends, you still had to trust them with your life. Even with your death. You literally put your hands in the hands of men who saw you as a number instead of 'Greg, a man of importance.' You followed their orders to go into harm's way even when you didn't understand why they wanted you to go there and you believed, at some level, that their 'word' was their bond. All that's commendable and I'd like to thank you, from the bottom of my heart, for everything you've done for me and my family and the country you and I share. I saw the Purple Heart on your license plate so I know you were injured at some point. You don't have to tell me how. But, I know you've made sacrifices I haven't had to make.

"Greg, the reason I take the time to talk to people like her (I nodded towards Janet) and you is because I know your life is precious. Personally, you and I don't know each other from Adam except for when we come in here. But, God does know you. He wants you to know Him. He's not only granted your wish of coming down and talking to people like you and me face-to-face, He's also taken care to have what He said to us written down and preserved. I know you'd like for Him to meet with you one-on-one and maybe He will. Maybe He won't. Maybe He's like your former Commanding Officer who expected you to carry out his orders even if he wasn't around to give them to you personally.

I believe that Jesus is the type of Commanding Officer who speaks to us in such a way that we can't help but understand His clear words of instruction. Further, I believe they come from the Bible. So, if you'd want to look into this 'hogwash' to see what's got someone like me, someone forty years younger than you, so bent out of shape and on fire, I'd be more than happy to get you a Bible and even suggest where you might want to start reading from it if you'd like."

For long, long, long, long minutes all you could hear was the sound of the machines in the room and the lady gently snoring. I had no idea what kind of impact I'd had on him and I had no idea if I'd offended him. Finally...

"I don't know about the Bible thing." He took off his hat and scratched a graying head. *"Would you mind if I chewed on this and asked you some more questions later? Then maybe I'll get a Bible."*

"That'll be fine." I said.

[Note: Approximately a month later I wrote the following as an update to my conversation with Greg.]

A note about Greg (my friend who claims he's an atheist)... The last time I saw him he actually introduced me to a couple of people he knew from cancer treatment. This is what he said: *"This is Lonnie. He's a pastor but he don't talk to you like most of them do."*

I can think of perhaps two or three dozen other ways I'd rather be introduced to someone but something must have clicked because there were several conversations started that day. I'll take anything that'll start a conversation.

[Note: A month later I wrote the following as a final update on Greg.]

As I told you, Greg and I have been able to have some quite spirited (pun intended) conversations about God, Jesus and the afterlife. Once I had gotten through his rough exterior (it wasn't hard to do – just a few hugs and he melted), I found out he's one of the nicest guys I've had the pleasure of getting to know.

Anyway, I had the opportunity to speak to him again a couple of hours ago and I've got some wonderful news. Greg, the once belligerent, almost always sarcastic man with a biting wit, who used to be an atheist (note the phrase 'used to be') is now our Brother (if you're a Christian)! Yep, he told me to my face that after he'd considered all I had told him and had confirmed much of what I'd said through other Christians, including his own brother and another minister at a church in Bay Minette, he'd accepted Jesus as his Lord and Savior. YAY!!!

I don't know about you but I personally think that's pretty neat! Greg is now attending Sunday School on a regular basis and says a lot of the questions he's had up until now are being answered. He also told me he's now telling everyone he can about Jesus and the fact that the Bible is true and the fact that people don't have to die and the fact that God is real! He used the word 'fact' quite a bit so I used it to illustrate my/his point. Again, YAY!!!

Since I wrote the last update on Greg (January 2008) he has gone home to be with our Lord and Savior, Jesus. The fact that Greg was a saint before he died thrills me to no end. Even better is that he faced death not with fear but, instead, with joyful expectation – an expectation I can personally promise you wasn't in vain. I'll be forever grateful God gave me the chance to get to know Greg before He died and that I know we'll be able to become true friends once we meet again in Heaven.

Chapter 23

If Christians Aren't Willing To Impress Others, Someone Else Will

One of the most important aspects of allowing Jesus to shine through us is the impact He (and we) can have on those in our world. I've seen it firsthand so many times I normally take it for granted that God will do amazing, sometimes miraculous things as long as we're willing to do whatever it is He has called us to do.

Some of the most amazing testimonies occur when God works through us when we don't expect Him to do so. However, I can assure everyone who reads this that you'll probably not ever have a great testimony to share with those you meet unless you're willing to act to benefit those in your own communities by sharing the love of Christ with others.

This is not to say that giving to missionaries who travel to places around the world most of us would be hard-pressed to pronounce and nearly impossible for us to locate on a map is wrong. It definitely isn't. I believe every single Christian should give as the Lord provides and prompts.

However, Christians MUST realize that ALL of us are called to be ambassadors of Jesus in our community. If we fail to recognize the *mission field in our own backyard* then we'll miss out on a tremendous opportunity to effect positive changes that could affect our entire culture. Unless you recognize that God has called YOU to be a missionary – regardless of your capacity to travel, your ability to speak, your level of education, your financial status or any other excuse – you won't step out in faith. In turn, you won't be blessed and those you meet (who might have been able to use a hug or a smile or a sandwich or a bottle of water or a shoulder to lean on) will have to wait until another Christian comes along who does understand that the Great Commission was given for them to fulfill.

Brothers and sisters, I urge you to act upon the faith God has placed inside of you (regardless of how small you think your faith is) so you can see, for yourself, the blessings He will bestow upon you when you help others. Kaylie, one of our 'volunteers,' wrote about an experience I believe aptly illustrates this.

Maria and McDonald's

"Hi Pastor Lonnie, I'm writing to tell you how much the last 99 for 1 Ministries newsletter impacted me and got me out of my 'Christian Comfort Zone.' You were quoted as telling everyone who volunteers with 99 for 1 Ministries: "*As a Christian, if the reason you don't give to others is because you're afraid you'll be taken advantage of, let me set your mind at ease. You WILL be taken advantage of. Period. Now that we've got out of the way, let's decide we'll give because Jesus (who most certainly holds the record of being taken advantage of before the cross, on the cross and after the cross) has given to us.*" I remembered you'd told this to me – almost word for word. The repeat of your advice in the newsletter convicted me BIG TIME! While I knew what you'd said was true and I wanted to live it out in my life, I hadn't been.

That all changed the day after I'd gotten your newsletter. I decided I was going to start doing for others regardless of how much I felt they 'might' take advantage of me. Here's what happened:

I met a lady downtown (where I work). She'd been standing outside of a McDonald's asking people for food. She was rail thin I knew in my heart that she *really wanted money* (probably for drugs or alcohol or cigarettes) but I decided I would buy her a meal. I went up to her and asked what type of meal she wanted. After looking at me as if I were from Mars she said, in quite broken English, that she wanted 3 burgers with ketchup only, a large drink and 3 orders of fries. To say that I was stunned wouldn't cover how I felt. Honestly, I thought about telling her 'Look, I'm not a bank...' but, instead, I smiled, went into the restaurant and ordered my lunch and hers.

I took her order to her, ask if I could pray for her (hoping that she'd understand some of what I was going to say – because of the obvious language barrier), she said 'Yes' so I did. I don't remember what I prayed but it was probably pretty lame.

Anyway, I smiled at her, gave her a quick hug (she smelled awful even from a few feet away) and went back into McDonald's to enjoy my lunch (and to think about 'what a good Christian I'd been this time').

Here's the good part: God has a way of putting us in our place just when we're up on our high-horse (at least He does with me). I sat down at a window so that I could watch Maria (that's the name she gave me) to see what she was going to do with the bag of food I'd bought her.

For a few minutes she just stood around, looking this way and that – almost like she was waiting for someone. Then, unexpectedly, she kind of jogged across the street and stopped near an alley. I saw her look into the alley and, apparently, she called out because, after a few seconds, three kids came out from behind a dumpster (they looked young – like 8, 10 and maybe 13) and walked up to her. Maria held the bag of burgers and fries out to them and they hurriedly dug-in. Maria stood with them for a few minutes, took one sip of the cold drink I'd bought her, gave it to the kids and then came back over to the corner where I'd found her. I'd completely stopped eating by this time and was kind of feeling sick to my stomach.

While I watched her begin the process of asking people for food all over again I had an inspiration. I called a friend of mine (Johnny) who I knew had a friend who worked at a local, downtown Christian shelter. Johnny and I talked for a few minutes and I told him the story I just related to you (only I think I talked a lot more than I'm writing).

Long story shorter, Johnny got in touch with Pennie who got in contact with her supervisor and they both met me at McDonald's. So that we didn't scare Maria it was decided that I would go out with Donna (the supervisor of the shelter) and talk to her. Again, long story much shorter, I found out that Maria had been beaten a few weeks earlier and had been thrown out of the apartment where she and her children had been living with her boyfriend (the guy who beat her). She and her kids had been on the street since then. Because she doesn't speak English very well she didn't know who to turn to so she and her kids had been staying in an abandoned building about a block away from McDonald's (I didn't even know the place existed) and she had been begging for food for her kids every day. Donna, who speaks Spanish fluently, was able to convince her to get her kids and to come to the shelter. In the past 2 days I've kept up with Maria (and Marcus, Mary and Josh – her kids) and found out the following:

Maria is a natural citizen of the U.S. (her parents were illegals who traveled where there was work so that's why she doesn't speak English very well), she'd been raped once (that's where Mary came from) and (this is where it gets GREAT), she's now enrolled to get her GED and is working at the SAME McDonald's where I met her at. Her kids are back in school and Maria hugs me every time she sees me.

Haha – talk about being blind and now seeing the light! Thanks be to God for all that 99 for 1 Ministries does – even through people like me (who don't listen well or learn all that fast). I know that I'll be taken advantage of by someone at sometime but, I also know that if I'd not stayed that day to eat lunch at McDonald's that I would have walked away thinking that Maria was just 'one of *those* people.' Now I know what type of person she is – a person Jesus loves, just like He loves me!"

Kaylie's testimony should be enough to convince us that if Christians aren't willing to impress others, someone else will. In Maria's case those who had impacted her life until the day she met Kaylie were people who only wanted to use her.

Another testimony that comes to mind about how we can show the love Christ in our community happened at an auto parts store.

Turn-Around Outreach at AutoZone

I was at AutoZone and I met Hazel – an elderly woman who reminded me of the lady in the 'Where's the Beef' commercials only she was African American not Caucasian.

Hazel is probably about 90 and she was at AutoZone to get oil for a car I'm pretty sure is older than I am. She and I arrived about the same time so I took my time getting out of my truck so I could hold the door open for her. She slowly climbed out of her front seat, opened the backdoor, took out a walker and made her way to the entrance. After she'd gotten inside I went around the store looking for some transmission fluid.

Hazel and I checked out at the same time so I hoisted the half dozen quarts of oil she had purchased and held the door open for her again. As I walked her to her car I asked if she wanted me to check the oil for her (at this point those of you who know me realize I was almost in over my head – checking oil is about as far as my mechanical expertise goes). She popped the hood of her car, I checked the oil and added a little of the same.

Just after I slammed the hood she asked me how long I'd worked at AutoZone because she wanted to tell my manager how nice of an employee I was. Once I'd explained that I wasn't an employee but a pastor of a semi-local church, a 15-minute conversation ensued.

During the conversation I found out her husband had died 5 years ago, two of her children had died a couple of years before and that she'd outlived some kind of exotic bird she'd gotten as a pet in the 1950's (it'd died a few months before). I also came to know that she was on a fixed income, that she and Mayor Sam Jones (the Mayor of Mobile, Alabama) were cousins and her favorite flavor of ice cream is cherry – don't ask me how that came up but it did.

As we closed our conversation I took her hand and prayed with her. Then I handed her a few coupons for free Chic-Fil-A chicken sandwiches.

Here's the cool part: She refused them! Hazel said, *"Honey, I appreciate this but there are a lot of other folks who need them more than me. Why don't you save 'em for those folks. Me and the Lord do all right. Here, when you find somebody who is hungry I want you to give them this."*

This little lady who was twice my age and living on only a few hundred dollars a month, handed me a five dollar bill. I was floored. We hugged and parted ways. An hour later I'd found a hungry person and they walked away with prayer, chicken coupons and a major financial blessing.

I'm telling you guys and gals... as Christians we should all be bragging about people like Hazel.

While I'm not certain of the actual author of the following quote, I read it in an article prepared by Ray C. Steadman (*The Christian and Worldliness*) and I think it's appropriate to this discussion in that it accurately depicts the way we, as Christians, should live in this temporal world.

"To sum up, the Christian's vocation is to be in the world, but not of it; to represent Christ in it and to intercede on its behalf because it is under judgment (this is the Christian's priesthood), to identify himself with its sufferings but not with its attitudes, to bring his influence to bear upon the world's life without being corrupted by the world's ways; to stand on the frontier, holding forth the Word of Life, and so to love and obey that Word that he has been delivered from the evil one and sanctified in the truth. Such a calling involves a cross. The man who separates himself from the world and seeks to escape it does not know the cross. The man who submits to the world's

pressures and loses his distinctiveness as a Christian does not know that cross. The man who seeks to be in the world, as our Lord was in it, but shows that he is not of it because he is a Christian and in Christ; that man will find his cross. It's only the disciple who follows Christ in both these respects who has a cross to take up."

I trust that anyone reading this intuitively understands why, from a Christian-perspective, the further away from Jesus a person is pulled, the worse it is for them. I also trust that any and all Christians who read this are ready to do whatever it takes (as long as it is moral and ethical) to show everyone why Jesus is more attractive than anyone or anything else in this world. But, before you can do this, it is imperative for you to learn how to 'walk the walk' and not just 'talk the talk' of Jesus.

A sobering fact is that unless we, as Christians, are 'on fire' (i.e., passionate) about the love of Jesus and we aren't afraid to live out our passion for Him, those around us will be attracted to someone or something that is infinitely less than the King of Kings and the Lord of Lords.

The following story is very personal in nature. It is an excerpt of an email that comes directly from my book Death, Heaven and Back. I've included it to illustrate how even the most seemingly mundane act of kindness, done in His love, can affect a person (sometimes an entire family). As you read the following, keep in mind that I was undergoing treatment for severe head and neck cancer and was unable to work.

The Impact of a Kind Gesture

"I'm writing today to express my gratitude because you, my brothers and sisters, allowed yourself to be used by God to bless my family.

When people are going through hard times, it's completely appropriate to remind them that 'God will provide.' What is sometimes forgotten is that He, more often than not, uses us as the instruments of His provision. What a fantastic honor!

While it's true I've pretty much been bed-bound because of severe headaches, nausea, and pain in general, I've also been able to beseech God and inquire of Him about several issues in my life and in the lives of others. The uninterrupted time I've been able to spend with Him has honestly refreshed me. Being in so much pain has enabled me to focus solely on Him and, while I'd rather not have had to go through this period of trial and tribulation, I'm really genuinely glad to have had His company.

My friends, I can say, without fear of contradiction, that YOU have also been a great source of release and refreshing for me. I've gotten lots and lots of snail mail and email notes, cards, and pictures (some from overseas), many from people I don't know. Those who have written have expressed words of comfort and concern for my family's spiritual, emotional and financial well-being.

My family has also been blessed by food – lots and lots of food. My kids probably think we've turned into some kind of restaurant. The food has been SUCH a blessing it's hard to overstate my thanks!

Knowing that Dawn hasn't had to worry about fixing meals for our family while I'm laid up (I usually do the cooking) has allowed me to rest easier.

But, one of the kindest gestures I've experienced thus far, happened today...

Two of my sisters-in-Christ delivered some foodstuffs to our home and took the time to pray for us. I was able to join them in this prayer and it was delightful to hear them say I really looked good with the exception that my throat seemed to have been on the losing side of a gang war.

After they left I noticed two small gift bags on the counter. Thinking they were for me, I peeked. They weren't for me. They were for my children! My heart leapt. I was speechless. I don't know from whom they came and it doesn't matter. The very fact that someone thought about my kids during all of this has made me nearly giddy.

My son, who wasn't in the room at the time, found the bags a few minutes later. His squeal of delight and that of his sister's told me they were joyous about the contents. He ran into my room not long afterwards and told me, breathlessly, that someone had brought them gifts. Via the prompting of God I inquired as to why he thought that was important. This is what he said, almost verbatim...

"Because somebody thought of my sister and me. They knew that maybe we'd be sad because of you being sick and they thought about how to make us happier too. That's what Christians are supposed to do, think of everybody, right?"

Too cool, eh?

Again, my thanks go out to whoever sent these gifts to my kids. Knowing that someone took the time to consider every part of my family makes me feel closer to every single one of my brothers and sisters in Christ (You). It also makes me proud to be a part of your family.

Chapter 24

How to Avoid Being a Hypocrite in the Eyes of God

I'm fully aware of the cautions of Matthew 6:1-6 which warns us "*not to do your 'acts of righteousness' before men to be seen by them*" and "*when you give to the needy, do not announce it with trumpets, as the hypocrites do in the synagogues and on the streets to be honored by men*" and "*when you pray, do not be like the hypocrites, for they love to pray standing in the synagogues and on the street corners to be seen by men.*" But, I'm also aware that we're called to feed the poor, take care of orphans and widows and to show love for our Christian brothers and sisters so the world will see that we're different and be drawn to Jesus. Since these things would be terribly difficult to do if we had to do everything covertly the warning found in Matthew 6 cannot be universally applicable to all that we as Christians do.

As we look at the construction of the Scriptures quoted above the word 'seen' stands out as the pivotal point in all of Matthew 6:1-6. I can't help but believe that the reason our attention is called to this word is because of what it implies. The word 'seen,' in Greek, is 'theatomi' which is similar to the English word 'theater.' The point I believe Jesus was making is that we shouldn't do things for people as if we were actors on a stage, vying for recognition of an audience, while pretending what we're doing is only for God. In modern language this is called 'posturing.'

Anyone who has ever seen a child throw a tantrum in order to get their way has seen posturing. A child's tantrum is designed to attract the attention of outsiders thereby making *themselves* the center of attention rather than their actions. As we get older, we become better able to disguise our posturing so that it often seems as though we're innocent of any wrongdoing and, in fact, are 'in the right.' If you follow politics or legal trials, I'm certain you can point to many instances of posturing regardless of what the issue happens to be.

Just as lawyers, politicians, corporate leaders, church members, children and you and I are guilty of 'playing to the crowd' in hopes of drawing positive attention to our cause, Jesus, in Matthew 6:1-6 says that those who do this aren't fooling the One Witness who will ultimately judge their actions – God. It is God who judges our actions (whether selfless or selfish) and it is He who rewards justly.

Of all the sins that Jesus rebuked, the one that receives His most scathing condemnation is that of hypocrisy. The entire chapter of Matthew 23 is reserved for His criticism. I think I can paraphrase the entirety of this chapter in eight words: *"Don't just talk the talk, walk the walk."*

So, if you are going to do something for God, JUST DO IT and don't wait for an audience to applaud you. Anyone who needs an audience before they'll do something (regardless of how small or grand the gesture) is guilty of practicing phony religion. This is something we, as Christians, should never countenance because those in the world will eventually see through those who are phony. But, more importantly, even if we're able to deflect suspicion from everyone (Christians and pre-Christians) for our entire life we must recognize that God will eventually judge that which we do.

If you're planning on living Jesus out loud, JUST DO IT!

Don't worry what anyone else thinks about what you do or even that anyone knows what you're doing… just do those things you know would please God and be happy that you're in His will. If you'll do this you'll not only divorce yourself from caring what the world thinks (which is a burden you don't want to have), you'll be rewarded by God because, rest assured, He sees and esteems what you do for Him in secret as righteous works.

Speaking of selfless acts, <u>ANYTHING we do that is selfless is for Him</u>.

Matthew 25:34-40, states: *"Then the King will say to those on His right, 'Come, you who are blessed of My Father, inherit the kingdom prepared for you from the foundation of the world. For I was hungry, and you gave Me something to eat; I was thirsty, and you gave Me something to drink; I was a stranger, and you invited Me in; naked, and you clothed Me; I was sick, and you visited Me; I was in prison, and you came to Me.' Then the righteous will answer Him, 'Lord, when did we see You hungry, and feed You, or thirsty, and give You something to drink? And when did we see You a stranger, and invite You in, or naked, and clothe You? When did we see You sick, or in prison, and come to You?' The King will answer and say to them,* **'Truly I say to you, to the extent that you did it to one of these brothers of Mine, even the least of them, you DID it to Me**.' *[Emphasis Mine.]*

Chapter 25

Ministering to Those Who Are Homeless

Two of the least hypocritical people I know are Melvin and Libby Badon. They're truly god-sends to those of us who need examples of what it's like to live a life wholly devoted to God and to one another. Together they've poured life into the lives of countless people. I consider them to be my Mom and Dad (even though my own mother is still alive and no one can truly take her place).

I highlight these two wonderful people up because they've been intimately involved in helping out people from all walks of life for over 50 years. I've asked Libby (Mom), who is in her 70's, to write about her experience when she volunteered with us as we ministered to a community of homeless people as well as to women who were trying to overcome drug and alcohol addiction. The reason I've asked her to do this is to show that you're never too old to do God's will.

[Note: Although Mom talks a lot about 'Lonnie doing this' and 'Lonnie doing that,' the thing I'd like you to notice is how many people were involved in the events I was led to set-up. It is truly humbling to be in the presence of such servants.]

"Serving the Under-loved" by Libby Badon

"Melvin and I already knew and loved Lonnie and his precious family years before he died. They were members of the church we attend. After dying and rising again, Lonnie, who we consider to be our son, began a new ministry – one he is well suited for… 99 for 1 Ministries.

Lonnie encourages everyone to be a part of servant evangelism projects regardless of the church they attend. As it happens, my daughters and I got very involved in the ministry to the women at the Haven of Hope. In fact, the very first time Lonnie went to meet the director of the Haven of Hope I went with him (along with Carolyn – a Social Worker who works directly with 99 for 1 Ministries). As it turns out, while neither Lonnie nor Carolyn knew either of the ladies in the director's office of the Haven, I knew both of them and had taught either them or one of their children in Sunday school years before.

I am thrilled to be part of a ministry that focuses most, if not all, its resources to serving those who are under-loved. I found out that the women who are clients of the Haven of Hope are ladies who have either abused drugs or alcohol (or both) and, in many cases, have been shunned by their husbands, boyfriends or family members. In other words, they are most certainly not genuinely loved enough.

Since my first introduction to the Haven of Hope through 99 for 1 Ministries I, along with many others, have enjoyed being a part of celebrating Christmas and Valentines with these wonderfully deserving ladies. Even when there was no special occasion (nothing celebrated by the world), Lonnie set-up times where we were able to minister to them. A great example is when he organized a 'Night of Pampering' for twelve ladies of the Haven of Hope.

My daughters and I, along with nearly 30 others (15 of whom were men), came together on a weeknight to celebrate life with these ladies by blessing them with massages, washing their feet, finger and toenail polishing and praying for them.

Lonnie made it clear that the men were only there to serve the women (all of us) by serving us a light dinner and desert and by toting water, towels and whatever else we needed. The only time the men were allowed to touch the ladies was if they (the ladies) offered to hug the men – even then Lonnie had strict guidelines so that there would be no semblance of impropriety. That night, I learned once again, how much Lonnie cares about people.

This was reinforced when, on a fall day in 2010, my daughter, Sharon and her son Hunter (12 years old) joined Lonnie and some others to go to Tent City. Just outside of downtown Mobile, right smack in the middle of the woods, we found and visited some lovely people. These men and women were living like primitives – they had no electricity, used a bucket as a bathroom, and were 'bunking' on cots and a couple of tents out in the open. Still, just as Lonnie said would be true, they met us with smiles on their faces. These precious people, most of whom are marginalized by society due to various factors, welcomed us and we sat with them and talked to them for a couple of hours. Hunter, my grandson, was asked to lead us in a Christian song and then we got to pray for each one.

After this we went to Bienville Square where we, again, found homeless people wandering inside the city. Just as we did in Tent City, we gave those we met (from a Korean War veteran to a lady who suffered from bi-polar disorder to an obvious drug-user) lunch bags of food, toothbrushes with toothpaste, water, Gatorade, canned goods with can openers and lots and lots of hugs and prayers. Even today, almost a year later, I can't forget those we met. They were so deeply appreciative.

God pulled us into a world we did not know existed for all practical purposes. But, because the Lord led us to meet all these delightful people, we'll never be the same!"

I think we'd all do well to remember that God can use everyone, at any age, to bless those He cherishes. All we have to do is step forward and say, 'Send me Lord.'"

Mom mentions that it was the fall of 2010 when I invited her to go with us to Tent City. What she didn't mention is that this was one of the first major outreaches I'd done for the homeless in Mobile, Alabama.

It was a remarkable day in that everyone who participated came away with such a dramatic redefinition of what homelessness really means to those who are in the midst of the same. Those who participated in this outreach met people who weren't criminals but who were outcasts from society surviving in an environment that is so disgustingly dirty and unsafe that even the most violent criminals in the U.S.A. wouldn't be allowed to live in.

Out of this single event, we've been able to put together over 4 dozen trips into Tent City. The 'Tent City Outreach' has become so well-known that college students and young professionals from other states have travelled to Mobile just so they can go with us and 'learn how to live Jesus out loud' to those who might not otherwise ever get a chance to see Him in action.

Our 'Tent City' outreaches have enabled us to get to know dozens of individuals we probably would've never come across had we not taken the first steps towards finding them.

Homelessness Is On the Rise

Homelessness in our society is no longer a phenomenon but a recognized 'trend' that is on the rise. This means that practically every city of more than 30,000 people has a 'tent city' of their own – regardless of whether or not such places are officially recognized. In America, the homeless population is estimated to be a staggering 3.5 million people (approximately 1.35 million of these are children – ages 0 - 18 years). Since these numbers are based solely on those utilizing government and reporting non-profit agencies, the actual number of homeless people is actually much higher.

Less than 8% of all those who are homeless have chosen this lifestyle. Another 25% or so suffer from mental illnesses (a percentage that also constitutes those who are addicted to illicit drugs and alcohol). The majority of those living 'on the streets' (i.e., in dumpsters, in alleyways, the woods, under bridges or in 'tent cities') simply can't afford permanent housing so they and their children must sleep outside. This means the _working homeless_ are becoming a reality in practically every city in the United States.

Recently I was interviewed by a student concerning the number of homeless people we're encountering as a ministry and as a society. I'm quoted as saying, "*Facts and numbers, especially when combined with repetition, seem to have a numbing effect on people. As humans we appear to have an innate desire to quantify things because doing so allows us to compartmentalize issues without being forced to confront the same. It's really a difference between 'knowing' and 'understanding' or 'sympathy' and 'empathy.' For instance, a person can intellectually know that there are over a million children who are homeless and even sympathize with their plight. But, until they emotionally understand the toll that such homelessness takes on these children, they won't be empathetic enough to do anything to help them. The reason is simple: sympathy requires little more than intellectual acknowledgement while empathy will almost always elicit an emotional and physical response.*"

The saddest part of ministering to the homeless is the fact that we, as a society, don't see them. Rather, we 'see' them, but we don't really see 'them' as people. In other words, when most people see someone holding a sign that says, 'Will Work For Food,' it's like they think "*If I give those people money they'll probably use it on alcohol or cigarettes*" instead of thinking "*I wonder how that person got to where they are now and how can I help them?*"

It's undoubtedly true that some of those who beg will use the money they acquire to buy tobacco and alcohol. But, my question is: *So what?*

Is their addiction any worse than the person who overeats or a teenager who spends ridiculous amounts of money on video games or a man who obsesses over a sports team or a woman who 'religiously' watches soap operas on television?

Statistically, for every one person you see standing on the street corner begging, there are fifty to one hundred people who are homeless and out of sight. Having talked and ministered to thousands of homeless people over the years I believe the reasons we don't see more of those who are homeless usually boils down to one of three things or a combination thereof:

1) People don't want to notice them. Remember my comment about quantification and compartmentalization? It's easier to deny that there's a problem than it is to admit a problem exists because, the moment you admit such a thing, you're obligated to make one of two decisions:

- Try and help figure out an answer to the issue.

- Ignore the issue as if it doesn't exist.

2) People who are poor (especially those who are homeless) don't want to be seen as outcasts. But, by and large, that's exactly how they're perceived. Intentionally or not we tend to group people and the situation we find them in as if they are one and the same. As such, those who are homeless have learned to blend into their surroundings so as to not be seen. That this is the case is directly attested to by the number of families who have seemingly normal lives during the day (they go to work and their children go to school) but, at night, they live in cars, in shelters, in abandoned homes or worse.

3) Finally, people who are homeless have found, through trial and error, that they can't trust the system of government agencies. This distrust has been fostered by generations of moments in which people could have done something for a family but, in the end, found it easier to let them 'fall through the cracks' of bureaucracy. Once a person who has virtually no hope learns that a system supposedly set-up to help them achieve some form of normalcy can't or doesn't work, they essentially give-up.

I truly believe the main reason we ignore homelessness as a real life issue is because it's ugly, messy and it doesn't coincide with what we want to think about.

Nothing about being homeless is pretty. From the mother who has to use a pair of dull scissors to cut the hair of her little girl short because she can't wash it more than once a week to the father and son who smell as though they've had to sleep in a dirty alley because that's exactly where they've slept for the past month. People suffering from skin disorders, multiple bug bites, hygiene issues (from not having toilet paper, toothbrushes, toothpaste or even clean water to regularly bathe) and more make us uncomfortable.

For just a moment imagine that you have a husband or a wife and you're trying to care for two or more kids under the age of 13 with just enough money to either get a room at a local motel or feed your family. Can you possibly fathom how hard this kind of life must be? Now, imagine being a child in that same situation. How frightened do you think you'd be if you were asked to go to sleep at night when you are, at best, surrounded by a room full of strangers in a shelter or, even worse, having to sleep in an alleyway or the woods in a tent? Imagine you're a child who realizes that if the authorities find out your family is homeless that you and your siblings could be taken away from your father and mother. Can you even imagine that kind of desperation?

Or, if you want to talk about those who have no children, try to envision yourself as having ingrown toenails because the shoes you wear are a size too small or that when you try to get a job people literally frown and turn away from you because of the way you smell or look. Compound all of this by the fact that you know this is reality – 24/7, 364 days a year. The reason I say 364 days a year instead of 365 is because there is a slim possibility that, during the Christmas season, you might be found by a 'good Samaritan' and given a present or two.

In my mind, the real question is: Is there an answer to homelessness?

In Matthew 26:11a Jesus said, "*The poor you will always have with you.*" With that in mind, we know there is never going to be a complete resolution to poverty. But that doesn't mean we shouldn't try to come up with a solution.

As unpopular as this idea is in certain progressive or liberal circles, if we were to teach the Biblical principles of 'getting a job (any job) and working as if you are working for Jesus Himself,' 'putting away a portion of what you earn and giving a portion of what you've earned back to Jesus,' 'families caring for other family members' and 'truly loving others like we love ourselves' then poverty, by and large, would be taken care of.

Of course, before any of this is going to take place we have to teach others that God should take center stage in your life. Once this is done then, I believe, most everything else would fall into place.

I truly believe that if we were to follow the advice of both St. Augustine and Martin Luther and live out this advice to the fullest extent of our ability that, both personally and as a society, we'd live in virtual paradise. Their advice was: *"Love God and do as you please."*

The point, of course, is that if we truly 'love God' then whatever it is we do will be done so that we please Him. Since God has given the church, His children, the mandate to teach the principles He set forth in the Bible that if we will follow through and do so, we will see a harvest of souls and a complete turnaround in societal woes. On the other hand, if we continue to abdicate the personal responsibility that God has given us to people who are paid to 'find solutions' we shouldn't be surprised when we become the modern day equivalent of indentured servants because we have relinquished our authority and have become willingly indebted to someone other than God Himself.

Fortunately, there are those who should be able to be trusted not to turn a blind eye to the needs we see that others have – the church (the body of Christ). As stewards of His grace and mercy we have to do our best to develop a sense of what others are going through. If you're called to minister to the homeless you'll quickly understand that homeless life is hard, often dangerous and always lonely and most of those you'll meet aren't homeless by choice – they are homeless despite their best efforts to make it in mainstream society.

For instance, Cindy, a resident at one of the Tent Cities in Mobile (there are five such locations in our area), suffers from bi-polar disorder and schizophrenia. I've gotten to know Cindy very well in the past couple of years and I can tell you she has a heart of gold. She doesn't drink, doesn't do drugs and she's one of the cleanest homeless people I've ever met. Still, because of her mental illnesses none of her family wants anything to do with her. I know because I've contacted all of them personally.

I hope the following testimonies encourage you to follow wherever our Lord leads you. The testimonies you are about to read come from a single outreach to those who are homeless (I've got at least a dozen more):

As we walked around a tent city talking to the residents, Margie literally stumbled into a member of our group. She had purposely gotten drunk early that morning and had specifically left the downtown area to get away from, as she called us, 'the God-people.' Fortunately, God knew where she was going and we happened to be there just as she arrived – much to her initial chagrin. Margie was extremely blunt (as most people who happen to be '3 sheets to the wind' are) in her distaste for anything 'godly' because her heart was hurting. The reason: She had just been told that her granddaughter had broken her neck and had died. Plainly and simply, she was mad at God.

No one who tried was able to effectively minister to her until, Carl decided to go and help her friend, David, work on getting a stump out of the ground so a tent could be erected. As Carl entered David's campsite they found Margie sitting there, all alone. For some reason, perhaps it's because of Carl's unassuming manner or, more than likely, because God had pricked her heart enough to see that through Carl's service to them he was a 'real Christian' Margie began to talk to him.

The conversation wasn't anything deep and moving – at least in the natural. In fact, to hear Carl tell it, it was a simple conversation about the book of Matthew. Margie told him that David often talked about the Bible to her and, when Carl asked what her favorite part was, she said, "*I like the book of Matthew.*"

It 'just so happened' that Carl had recently completed a study on Matthew and was able to talk to her about Levi. Levi, a man so named by his parents because they hoped he would become a priest but who had squandered this opportunity, was shunned by the religious leaders of his day. Then, Jesus Christ, a priest of the Highest Order, stepped on the scene and changed Levi's life. Levi, of course, is better known as Matthew. After talking with Margie (once Carl had left) I found out she had taken from their exchange that "*Jesus loves her and everyone else.*" PRAISE GOD!

Another gentleman, Ken, told me, as I was drinking a bottle of water and watching James Buck and his son mow a field of knee-high grass, he was '*amazed that so many of you Christians had come out to help when most people are at home or at the beach.*' I've known Ken now for awhile and I can tell you from having heard his testimony, he has been through the wringer when it comes to people who profess Christianity but who don't practice what they preach.

Ken put his arm around me and said, in a very low voice – as if there was someone standing really near to us who might overhear him – "*Pastor, y'all are the real deal and I want you to know that if there is ever anything I can do for y'all all you have to do is ask.*" I smiled and hugged him... all the while thinking to myself '*Ken, you just did something for me... you've told me that you know that Jesus is alive and working through all of those that are here today.*'

A married couple we met work 40+ hours a week and are homeless because the husband lost his job a few months ago. They missed a couple of mortgage payments, couldn't catch-up and they lost their home. I was told that they'd soon be moving away from Tent City into an apartment because, living in the woods has allowed them to save enough money to afford a 'roof over their heads' instead of canvas.

Amazingly, this couple and two others who live in Tent City, routinely go to other homeless camps around the city and serve their peers (i.e., others who are homeless). Think about that for a minute. Here are 4 people who have practically nothing in this world and, yet, they are willing to go out and share whatever it is that God has provided with others who are, in their words, '*really having a hard time.*'

C'mon! If these people, who live in the woods, being bitten by bugs, fending off thieves and who have no electricity, no showers, no vehicles and the only roof over their heads is a two and a four man tent, aren't '*really having a hard time*' how in the world can I ever complain about anything? I think about this kind of stuff every time I type a message on a computer that is sitting in my dining room, cooled by central heat and air, while I'm sipping on an ice cold glass of tea! Sheesh! What a BLESSED man I am!

Finally, Tim, a tall, very happy-go-lucky man whom I've known for a few weeks gave His life to Christ as Pastor Nathan and others ministered to him. The yells of triumph over Satan because of this man's changed nature from our group actually brought others out from their tents to 'make sure everything was okay.' Haha!

It was a wonderful end to a beautiful day.

Thanks be to God Almighty that He has allowed us, those He calls His children, His brothers and sisters and His friends (co-heirs in the Kingdom of God), to go and minister to those who are so marginalized that they are either forgotten or ignored by mainstream society.

I am SO proud of those who allowed me to serve with them and of those who put together sandwiches, bought drinks and fruit and gave to 99 for 1 Ministries to make this possible. But, more than anything I'm so very, very happy that God loves me enough to surround me by His disciples who showed me that they love him with every drop of sweat they shed and every smile and laugh they shared today.

My questions to you are:

"What are you willing to do to help those who are homeless"

and

"Would God be pleased with your answer?"

I am absolutely humbled and amazed that God has allowed us to be a vital part of helping over a dozen families and a couple dozen individuals find permanent housing, full-time employment and around fifteen men and women get into drug rehabilitation programs.

As I leave the issue of homelessness and turn to other issues I would like to say that while I realize that outreaches to the homeless is definitely not for everyone, if you're ever involved in the same, your life will be forever changed.

Chapter 26

Ministering to a Person Who Is Ill or Who Is Undergoing a Stressful Situation

Having spoken to many people who've gone through major illnesses and came out on the other end alive and well I can tell you that family and friends (those whom you know love you) often say things that are completely insensitive.

Imagine getting a message akin to this: *"I feel badly that I didn't contact you sooner because I know so much about natural health and nutrition. The reason I feel bad is because so many people are so naïve about what actually causes* [add the name of whatever illness you're combatting here] *and how to get rid of it naturally. I know you chose to take the medical route, to have an operation to remove whatever it was that invaded your body and then to take drugs to kill the rest of it, and it isn't and wasn't necessary. But, I understand that people get scared and don't know of any other alternatives."*

In essence, what's being said is that the person failed to consider all the alternatives at their disposal before subjecting themselves to surgery and subsequent treatments for the affliction they had to deal with. Regardless of whether or not this is true, an elderly friend of mind used to say something I think is applicable: "*Once milk is spilled, clean it up – don't tell the person how dumb it was to spill it in the first place.*" In other words, once a decision has been made the time for advice is over. Instead of telling a person how dumb they were (in your opinion) for making the decision, help them deal with the aftermath of the same.

A word of advice I'd like to give anyone who knows someone with any type of illness (especially one that is life-threatening) is to be less sympathetic and more empathetic to the person you're dealing with.

In counseling, one learns that to be sympathetic is to *'maintain a distance from another's feelings'* while to be empathetic means to *'understand or imagine the depth of a person's feelings.'*

Almost no one likes sympathy but almost everyone craves empathy because it means to have feelings *with* a person rather than feeling sorry *for* a person. In essence, when someone is being empathetic towards me, it means they are willing to *walk a mile in my shoes.*

I can personally attest to the healing and calming power of conversation – especially for someone facing death. Believe me, I never expected anyone to fully understand what I was going through when I had cancer and was undergoing treatments for the same. Still, it was fantastic when someone showed me enough kindness to simply sit down and talk.

I encourage you to not be all that concerned with how the conversation is going to go. You aren't going to be expected to give any life-changing advice and, normally, the conversation you'll have won't even be morbid. In fact, most of the conversations I had with people who were willing to talk with me were very life giving. I've found that the majority of people who are faced with life-threatening disease aren't all that interested in discussing death or even the afterlife. What we all want (whether sick or well) is to feel normal and part of normalcy is to talk about things that interest us.

So, if you're willing to enter into the life of someone who is ill, keep the following notes in mind:

▪ Pray, pray and pray some more. Pray before you go, pray when and if they ask you to for them or their loved ones and pray after you've left. If you're asked to pray use simple words and just talk to God because that's what prayer is. When you pray, you need to believe that God has the power to heal but you should also be willing to accept it if He doesn't. Believe me when I tell you that prayer really does move God.

▪ Smile. A lot.

▪ Be patient with those of us who are ill.

▪ If you're nervous about speaking to someone, bring along something to do with your hands such as a book (non-religious is best unless you know the person very well), a deck of playing cards, a checkerboard, etc. so you don't fidget.

▪ It's important to eliminate distractions (loud music or television programs, rowdy children) so that you and the person you're speaking with can have real, meaningful conversations. This doesn't mean that you should chitchat just for the sake of avoiding silence. Remember that silence is okay and often just making yourself available to the person is enough support.

▪ Understand that anyone who is ill will probably have wildly varying levels of energy at different times. As such, you should allow them to dictate the length of time you visit and converse. Ask them to let you know if they need to rest and be alert to visual signs that they're getting tired.

▪ Allow the person to express their feelings (even if these feelings include guilt, depression, anger, or fear). Always keep in mind that these feelings aren't caused by you even if they are directed at you. Also remember that your 'job' is to listen and empathize with the person. They aren't really looking for someone to give them answers, they just need a friendly shoulder to cry on and someone they can trust not to get offended if their behavior seems a tad abnormal.

• Don't be afraid to ask the person about their recovery or treatment options. People often like to talk about the options they have because it gives them a sense of control. Of course, if they don't want to talk about these things, don't pursue the matter.

• As you get to know the person (or anytime you feel led by the Lord), ask the person if they need or want you to contact anyone to tell them what's going on. This can be an especially helpful offer since some people put off contacting friends or family until it's too late. Offering to be a go-between may challenge the person to be honest about who he or she needs or wants to contact and it can alleviate much of the stress of them having to make the initial contact.

• Ask about their life, what they've done thus far and what they plan to do in the future. In other words, get them to reminisce and imagine a future. Don't be shocked if this type of talk brings one or both of you to tears – and don't be afraid to cry in front of them!

• And last, but not least, don't visit when you're ill and don't smoke around a person who is ill!

A case in point that illustrates how well-meaning friends can be either helpful or burdensome comes from a lady I know personally. Jennifer lost a child around five years ago (at the time this book was published). A blog entry she made demonstrates some of the same principles I've just put forth.

Advice From a Grieving Mother

"Today is the anniversary of the worst day of my life and like all anniversaries good or bad I feel like I have to look back and reflect. Before I lost a child I admit I had no idea about the devastation and emotional chaos you are thrust into. I feel like most 'normal' people are thinking, "*Geez woman, it's been five years! Get over it already!*" Still I feel that five years on this crappy road have yielded some wisdom.

Get a sense of humor because you never know when you will really need it.

Life is brutal. Need some examples? Turn on the news and hear about teenagers being gunned down because of the color of their skin, children starving around the world, mass murders and human trafficking. Examples are all around us. People cut you off in traffic, neighbors can be rude and family members can be the cruelest of all. Material for a comedy routine? Probably not, but if you can find even the smallest ways that life, though brutal, can be absolutely hilarious you will be far more psychologically healthy than most.

People said some of the rudest things after we lost Leo. I choose to believe they were being ignorant and not intentionally cruel, but if I hadn't found ways to chuckle at their stupidity then you probably would have read about a crazed grief stricken mother slapping someone into the next zip code. Life is hard. Bad things will happen and learning to laugh at the ridiculous that surrounds us can save you from doing 10-20 in a penitentiary. That leads me to my next discovery...

If you think you might say something stupid just shut up and give a hug instead.

People say dumb things all the time. Normally this isn't too big of a deal but if you're dealing with someone who just lost a child you could be inflicting serious damage.

"*I know just how you feel.*" Nope, not unless you've also lost a child. The death of your 95-year-old grandmother, your third cousin, your next door neighbor, or your goldfish doesn't compare.

Parents will probably die before you. Spouses could possibly die before you. But your child? This goes against everything normal and natural in the world. We have words like "orphan" and "widow," but is there a word in our enormous dictionary for parents who lose a child? None. It defies description.

241

"God took your child because they were too perfect/ beautiful/ sweet." Whoa, whoa whoa! The God that I believe in is not so cruel or heartless that he would kill off a child because they were apparently an awesome example of babyhood. Countless scholars and theologians have spent centuries debating the nature of God without firm answers, so unless you have a personal hotline where God gives you answers to questions that have puzzled man since the dawn of time then its best to just be quiet.

You aren't Houdini so don't pull a disappearing act.

One of the most amazing phenomena I have seen is how people you thought would be there for you no matter what suddenly vanish from your lives after you lose a child. Or maybe they see you from a distance and suddenly avoid contact or reverse direction.

What they're probably thinking is, *"I just don't know what to say."* Perhaps they figure a phone call would be too intrusive or bothersome so they never dial your number again. As irrational as it might be, I think, deep down, many feel like the level of sadness and despair a grieving parent is immersed in might be transferrable so they avoid it at all costs.

Conversely, people you barely knew or had little contact with or you suspected were schmucks will step up and show a depth of caring and compassion you didn't know was possible. These sweethearts will genuinely restore your faith in humanity. Before this tragedy hits someone you know, decide whether you're going to be a schmuck or a sweetheart.

It doesn't get better, but it does change.

Let's pretend for a minute you're driving down the road listening to some awesome tunes on the radio. The weather is perfect... nothing but clear skies ahead. In a split second, without any warning, a huge semi broadsides you and your life is changed forever. You wake up in the hospital surprised to be alive, but then discover you have been permanently paralyzed and will spend the rest of your life in a wheelchair.

You spend months and years just learning how to navigate in a world that looks familiar but is now filled with challenges at every turn. Five years later is it better? Well, yes and no. At this point you've learned how to get around. You've learned how to integrate the pain into your life. You've accepted that your life will never be *normal* again.

Much like someone who suddenly loses the ability to walk, I've discovered how to get around, how to function and how to let the pain be a part of my life, but not consume my life. It certainly isn't better, but I am thankful that it's different.

My marriage is amazing!!!

One of the other things the schmucks liked to bring to my attention after Leo died was how often couples who lose a child wind up divorced. From personally getting to know hundreds of families whose marriages remained intact after the death of a child I find this statistic inaccurate. However, let's review what Darrin and I have been through in the past five years:

▪ Losing a child unexpectedly before we even celebrated our first anniversary.
▪ Losing our business.
▪ Subsequent extreme financial hardship.
▪ Continued legal battles with my ex-husband.
▪ Raising two teenage girls.
▪ All the inherent bumps, bruises and difficulties that go along with a second marriage.

And through it all we have stood strong! Pardon me while I do a victory lap for that one. I am really proud of us!

God doesn't mind the tough questions.

Ok, here comes the big, ugly confession. Are you ready? After Leo died I was really angry at God. I don't mean slightly peeved. I am talking about deep down, gut wrenchingly, angry!

I had been through one of the worst divorces ever and had just managed to meet a decent guy and was all ready to enjoy a little of the good life. For what? To get the rug yanked out from under me in the cruelest possible way? Why would God do this? Haven't we all heard stories of people near death that were somehow saved in ways that could only be termed miraculous? OK, so where was my miracle? Wasn't Leo destined for great things? Give me one good reason why a seemingly healthy baby could go down for a nap and, with no explanation, just never wake up?

I spent quite awhile furious at the Almighty. I stopped reading my Bible and stopped going to church. However, there was one thing I didn't stop. I never stopped talking to God. Often the conversations were pretty one-sided with a lot of demanding on my part. (*"How could you? Why did you? Explain yourself!"*) Sometimes they were pleading. (*"Please, please, please give me back* my son. I'll *do anything, give you anything, be anything!"*)

Did I then or do I now think I was being sacrilegious in any of these prayers? Not even a little. God understands my pain and I discovered that he loves me more than I can even grasp. For now that is enough. The final and most important thing I've learned is the answer to the request I asked of God the night Leo died....

Lord, where are You in all of this?

I should have buckled my seat belt for the answer to this one. God answered me that night and has answered me continuously over the past five years. So where is God in all this?

He's in the people who rushed to be with us in the ER that awful night. In the many practical good deeds people did in the months after we were consumed with just trying to get from one day to the next. He's in all the friendships I've made with other 'Angel Moms' who are always ready to listen and truly understand. He's in the sweethearts who have made Darrin and I feel surrounded by love on that awful day.

And my personal favorite... a box of cupcakes and cookies left by my front door. Is God in a cupcake? You bet He is when it's given out of love and compassion. God has shown me that I am blessed beyond comprehension because I am surrounded by people who want to make it just a tiny bit better.

Isn't that where God is for all of us? We can all agree that the world can be horrible, unfair and cruel, but if we allow God to use us to show His love and compassion we can help make the world a little less hard to get through. Really, that is the secret for us all whether we have lost a child or not. Healing from any pain can come, but only to the extent that we are willing to reach out and love others."

Chapter 27

Get Outside of the Four Walls of Your Church

As much as I'd like to say that churches around the world are falling over themselves to promote or, at least, support outreaches such as those done by 99 for 1 Ministries, I can say, without fear of contradiction, that most of them aren't.

The primary reason for the lack of concentrated outreach is, in my opinion, a lack of emphasis by the Senior Pastor. This is not to say that the Senior Pastors are wrong in what they emphasize – in fact I support whatever it is that they want to concentrate on because they are the ones who are supposed to listen to what God says and to lead the flock Jesus has given to them. But, I want to caution anyone who wants to really invest in outreach programs such as the ones you've read about… <u>you may be doing this all by yourself</u>.

It's been my experience that pastors, especially those who either don't have the luxury of getting outside the four walls of the building they're in or who simply don't want to invest any more energy than they already are, or don't 'see' the importance of outreach – at least as it concerns growth for their own church. Instead of going out into the highways and hedges to invite others to join the Kingdom of God regardless of which church those they meet begin attending, most pastors are only interested in doing activities that reap fruit for their own particular congregation.

Now that I've made the above statements allow me to plainly clarify my position so I'm not taken out of context by well-meaning Christians. Do I think servant evangelism should be part of every church in every community in the world? Yes. Do I think every church that doesn't focus part of their energy, money, time, prayer and volunteer hours towards outreach is wrong for not doing so? No. Again, I sincerely believe that each and every corporate church should be led by a pastor who seeks counsel from God and those He has put in their path as to what a particular flock should be doing.

So, in short, if the corporate church you go to hasn't caught 'outreach fever,' it's okay. It may be that God will use you to infect those in the church you attend with the bug He's given you. If not, that's okay too! Since you are the Church (i.e., the body of Christ), He will work with you and all the other churches (i.e., other believers) you come in contact with to help you minister to those you have a heart for. If that means you have to partner with believers who attend other churches, GREAT. If not, GREAT. Either way, you win, those you serve win and God wins! It's the perfect trifecta.

Frankly, I don't think the Lord cares one iota where a person attends church (be it in a conventional church building, a home, a tent or in the most far-flung swamp in the world) because Jesus tells us in Matthew 18:20 "*For where two or three are gathered in my name, there am I among them.*" If His Word is taught, unadulterated, and those He loves are served, then I can't imagine He would ever be disappointed despite the differences in congregational styles.

I believe it was Steve Sjogren who said something akin to: '*Servant evangelism serves the church by raising the spiritual water level wherever it is done.*' If it wasn't Steve then I apologize to whoever it was. This analogy is appropriate because when water is added to a lake the level of the same rises equally on all sides and when Christian outreaches are done within a community ALL churches benefit because Christians (en masse) are seen in a different light. The more who participate the brighter the light of Jesus becomes.

If you're like me then you've heard, time and time and time again, that, in order to be effective stewards of the love of Jesus, we need to step outside of the four walls of our church and go into the world. While you may have heard this so often it seems cliché, I assure you it's not.

Jesus' ministry didn't take place only in synagogues. Rather, He, through His disciples took the Gospel Message far and wide into the world. Since the implied and explicit instructions we're given in the Bible are to follow the example of Christ this means going to where people *are* rather than waiting for them to grace our doorsteps.

I've tried to give you an idea as to what ministry can look like if it doesn't occur inside the building in which you worship. For the most part, the examples I've given you have been tame. Now I'd like to introduce you to one of the most 'out there' type of ministries I've ever been part of – at least as far as I collected some of the items needed to do what was suggested – not that I actually participated in the actual ministry itself.

When I tell people that the time I spent in California gave me my primary introduction as to what living Jesus out loud is like, a lot of Christians think I'm joking. But, it's true. It was while living in California I learned to go to wherever pre-Christians are and to present the Gospel in a way that challenges them to see Jesus in a different light than they may have ever done in the past.

The following story illustrates how we, as Christians, can take back territory that has either been claimed by Satan or surrendered to him and, in doing so, we can be used by our Lord to free those held captive by sin. Unfortunately, Christians I've talked with would never even dare to suggest this type of evangelism project to the members of their church because it almost sounds sacrilegious.

With that being said, here's the story as it was related to me – I've since verified the accuracy:

Washing the Feet of Dancers

Years ago my wife and I attended a church whose pastors had fully bought into the concept of serving their community. The church was located in the center of over a dozen 'strip clubs' (clubs where women dance either semi-nude or completely nude) and well over twenty establishments that served alcohol to their patrons. To most, this wouldn't be considered the best spot to plant a church. Still, God had provided the building to our congregation and we were determined to make the best of the situation.

A few months after we'd moved in about thirty members met to talk about ways we could influence our city in a mighty way for God. Normal ideas such as doing a Ten Commandment Challenge (in which anyone who is able to quote (even semi-accurately) one of the Ten Commandments gets a free soft drink, bottle of water or snack), collecting food items and distributing them to needy families, etc. were discussed. All the projects had merit but Selma, a seventy-something lady (a grandmotherly type with the blue and white hair who you'd suspect spent her time knitting and rocking away her twilight years) came up with a novel suggestion – at least it was novel to everyone there.

She asked, *"Can I ask a few of our women if they'd mind helping me wash and massage the feet of the ladies who dance in the strip clubs in our area?"*

Her rationale was that *'their feet must be awfully sore and as much as I like my feet rubbed, I can't imagine how appreciative they would be.'*

Talk about silence. For a moment or two you could have heard a pin drop on our upstairs, carpeted Sunday school rooms. Then we all burst out laughing until we realized Selma was being absolutely serious.

A young man voiced what most of us had been thinking: *"What would the people in the others churches in our area think about us going into a strip club and actually helping women who do something God doesn't approve of?"*

As soon as the question was posed we had our answer. Almost simultaneously, I and another asked: *"What do you need for the outreach?"*

It wasn't that we disagreed on whether or not God disapproves of dancing half-naked in order to inflame the senses – He most certainly does – but, rather, our knowledge that Jesus was criticized for going to the houses of sinners made us determined to follow His lead. The idea of 'invading a house of ill repute' may sound counterintuitive, possibly counterproductive to the message of Christ or even just plain stupid, but wait until you read the outcome.

The list of materials needed for the outreach was simple:

- Tubs to hold warm water
- Epsom salts
- EZ Disinfectant to clean tubs after each use
- Pumice stones (easily the most expensive item because they shouldn't be used on more than one set of feet – we found small stones for around 50¢ each.)
- Towels (lots)
- Massage oils
- 1 connection card per dancer

There were over twenty strip clubs in a four miles radius around our church so finding a manager to talk to wasn't difficult. Selma took the lead and, along with four other women from our church (ranging in age from 22 – 56), began going to each individual 'gentleman's club,' asking to speak to a manager and explaining what they wanted to do.

The first nine club managers turned them down flat. 'No way. No how. Not gonna happen.' The tenth club was different. It was owned and operated by a woman who took time to ask our ladies why they wanted to do what they planned on doing, if they were going to proselytize her dancers and if they were going to be offended at the dancers lack of attire. Selma gave the following answers:

1. "We just want to do something kind for the ladies because we know they work really hard and because it's something we think Jesus wants us to do."

2. "No. We won't proselytize your ladies although if they ask us why we're offering to massage their feet we'll tell them the same thing we just told you – that we know they work hard and because it's something we think Jesus want us to do. If they have any further questions we'll give them a connection card that has our church number and the following statement: 'We love you, Jesus loves you. No strings attached.'"

3. "We are fully aware of what your ladies do for a living and we won't be shocked by anything they wear or don't wear or any kind of language they choose to use."

According to Selma, after a few more minutes of discussion concerning respecting the time each of the dancers had between numbers, not being pushy, etc., the owner gave them permission for the outreach.

For obvious reasons, no guys were allowed to participate in the actual outreach itself.

Cindy, one of the ladies who attended the first seven outreaches, which were done on consecutive days (starting on Sunday), had this to say:

"The first day we arrived at a club around 3 p.m. and set-up well behind the stage. It took us almost 30 minutes just to get everything ready to serve the first dancer because our nerves were on edge. The reason we were nervous is because we didn't know what to expect in terms of our acceptance in an obviously foreign arena. Plus, they'd all been staring at us like we were aliens. After we were set-up it was time to start introducing ourselves to all the dancers.

I talked to the first dancer, Candy (I found out this wasn't her real name but, at first, I was naïve enough to think it was), and said something like, "*Hi my name is Cindy and we're here to massage your feet when your through dancing.*" She inquired as to why and I replied, "*Because Jesus told us to.*"

She rolled her eyes at me and said something that began with a foul four-letter word and ended with the word 'off.' I was so completely shocked I just stood there watching her walking away.

It wasn't her language that shocked me but, rather, her attitude. I was shocked because I was so used to people being attracted to the notion that Jesus might have actually asked us to do something that when she seemed offended it simply didn't compute. Looking back and putting myself in her place I can understand what I must have sounded like. I'm fairly certain I'd have had the same response (minus the language) to a pastor who came to me holding snakes and telling me: "*Jesus said to play with poisonous snakes as a sign of our faith.*" It's actually quite funny to me now but, at the time, I was mortified I'd failed so miserably.

The nice thing about being the first one who fails is that everyone else is given a bit of a comfort zone. Unfortunately, the next seven women we tried to introduce ourselves to had, for all practical purposes, the same response as I did. Finally, Selma, who I swear had never done anything like this stepped into the fray and showed all of us 'young-uns' how to do it.

Selma approached a dancer who'd just finished dancing and who we'd not yet introduced ourselves to and said, "*Hi, my name is Selma. Darlene, the owner of the club, said that her girls might like to have a foot massage after you've danced. So, if you'd like one just follow me over here.*" She didn't wait for the dancer to say anything but, instead, she nodded towards our 'massage station,' touched the young lady on her shoulder and led her to a waiting chair.

The rest is history. ALL of us adopted Selma's example and soon all our chairs were full. For the next six hours we massaged the feet of ladies who were as young as 19 and as old as 38. The ladies started introducing us to the other dancers – one of whom introduced us as being "*Those ladies from some weird church up the street.*"

As we washed and massaged over a dozen pair of feet, somewhere along the way we learned where they came from, what had brought them to their current place of employment, their real names verses their stage names (and why they or their manager had chosen the stage names), how many children they had (most had two or more children although I learned that one of them wasn't able to have kids because she'd been severely beaten by an ex-boyfriend) and much more.

It was incredible! Once the first lady (the one Selma had gotten to get a foot massage) was done and started telling everyone how nice her feet felt, it seemed like no one could wait to get their own feet done. Honestly, after awhile, it became almost exactly like a 'girl's night' – although the language was more colorful and there was less clothing than any of us were used to. We started packing up around 9 p.m. and, as we left we were almost attacked by the ladies who wanted to hug all of us. They asked when we'd be back the next time, if they could pay us for our services (of course we said 'No'), and a couple of them even asked what church we went to because '*any church who would do something like this in a strip club must be really cool.*'"

Selma and the same group of ladies went back to the same club seven more times. On day five the owner of the club came to them as they were getting their stations ready and told them (paraphrased): "*I want to thank you for being so kind to my girls. All of them have told me that they can't believe ladies from a church are doing this for them.*"

To make a very long story much shorter, three years after Selma introduced this radical idea, nearly 100 women in our church and other churches had participated in the outreach *and* there wasn't a single strip club around the church.

But, the story doesn't end there.

Simultaneous to the massage idea, we men, not wanting to be outdone, decided to develop an outreach that'd be directed towards those who frequented the bars in our area. Taking an idea from a very popular outreach we'd previously done, we rented two hotdog stands, and had a bright, backlit sign made that read: "**Soft Drink & Hotdog .50¢.**" One of the guys in our church knew how to get a vendors license and, in about two weeks, we were ready to go.

We began placing the stands directly across and in front of the bars in our area. When the guys and gals who frequented those establishments came out (night or day), they'd see our brightly colored sign and we'd engage them in small talk and a sales pitch that went something like: *"C'mon over! You gotta be hungry. Get 50¢, a hotdog, all the fixings and a soft drink before you leave."*

When people came over and ordered their hotdog and soft drink they were also given two quarters. This threw people for a mental loop. Some people, who weren't so inebriated they couldn't do the math, objected – thinking that we must have thought they'd already been paid and were giving change back.

But, once our men (all of whom wore 'Christianese' T-Shirts with slogans on them such as *'Feel taken advantage of? Imagine how Jesus feels!'* and *'To know Me is to love Me: Jesus!'*) explained that they were just there to serve people, life changing chats often ensued.

One of the most memorable talks happened at around closing time. Brian, a former police officer and one of the most dedicated guys who ever wrangled a hotdog, relates the story:

"It was a Friday morning and David and I had just set-up our hotdog stand. We'd never been to this particular bar before so we didn't know what to expect. Most of the time people who came out of the bar at closing time were so drunk that I'd walk over to them, direct them over to our hotdog stand and, while they ate or talked or ranted and raved, I'd call a taxi cab for them and send them on their way home. The cab company was operated by a really good friend of ours who happened to be a Messianic Jew and he'd kindly offered to give anyone who was drunk a free ride home as long as we could get them to accept it. This ended up being really good for everyone – people got home safely, other people weren't put in danger because of a drunk driver, the police officers in the area really appreciated it and the cab company got a lot of free publicity.

Anyway, I was almost in the middle of the street, about half way between the hotdog stand and the bar when I saw this older gentleman come out of the bar. As usual I spoke directly to the man and asked if he'd like a hotdog and a coke before he went home. To my surprise he stopped in his tracks and stared back and forth at me and the hotdog sign behind me. Without any warning whatsoever, the guy just bursts out in tears. I mean, he was really crying. Sobbing like crazy.

For a moment I didn't do anything. While I'd encountered people who cussed me out, who flipped me off, who laughed at me, who gladly came over to get a drink and something to eat, who wanted to know what kind of business we had and everything in-between… I'd never had someone simply stop and cry.

After what seemed like a couple of minutes to me I finally got my feet moving and I went over to the man to see if I could call him a cab. I thought to myself, *"Man, this guy doesn't even need to get near his car."*

As I got close enough to him to touch him, I reached out and kind of placed my hand on his shoulder and then he did something else that shocked the living daylights out of me. This man, a guy I'd never seen before in my life and who I was certain was about three sheets to the wind, grabbed hold of me, wrapped his arms around my chest and back, buried his head in my chest and just started wailing. I'm talking about blubbering, snot-flying, shoulder-heaving wailing. I just stood there on the sidewalk holding him and half-expecting him to pass out at any moment.

David finally joined me and, together, we got the man to the side of the street where our hotdog stand was. As I sat down with the guy on the curb, waiting for his tears to subside, David called a cab. They were busy that evening so David was told we'd need to keep the man there for at least a half hour. The way the guy was crying I didn't think that'd be a problem at all.

Ten or fifteen minutes later the man finally stopped crying. Having been with him for over twenty minutes at this point I'd had time to size him up. He didn't have the same 'look' about him that most of the people we ministered to did. I couldn't quite put my finger on it but there was something different about him. It wasn't his clothes or his age or his hair or even the fact that he didn't reek of alcohol – this fact, in and of itself, surprised me because I would have sworn on a stack of Bibles that this guy had at least twice the legal limit of alcohol in his system. I didn't know what it was until he began to speak. This is what he said as best as I can remember:

"I can't believe you guys are here." David and I looked at each other after he made this comment and I kind of shrugged as if saying 'I don't know what he means either.' *"You see, I'm a pastor from [another church] about an hour from here. I've been coming to this bar now for about six weeks because I thought no one would find me here but then the two of you show up."*

To say David and I were shocked at this revelation would be like describing a lightning bolt as an electric spark. I don't know about David but I was floored. He'd started crying again but after a minute or two he'd calmed down enough to where he could talk again.

I asked, *"What do you mean 'the two of you?' Do we know you?"*

He looked up at me, snot dripping from his nose and laughed. He actually laughed. *"No, we don't know each other but God knows us all."* He must have seen the looks of confusion on our faces because he explained, *"You're both Christians aren't you?"* We silently nodded. *"I knew it as soon as you asked me if I wanted a hotdog. You see, I've heard of a church that does this but I never thought I'd see someone out this late at night. But, here you are and here I am. I guess God wanted me to get caught, didn't He?"*

As it turned out this man was the senior pastor for a fairly large church. He and his wife had been having marital trouble and, because he was supposed to be a 'man of God' (which he is) he didn't think he'd be able to find anyone to talk to. So, he turned back to what he'd leaned on years before he became a pastor: alcohol. It just so happened that that night God had us there for our brother.

David called the cab company back and cancelled the taxi, we folded up the stand and, while David followed us, I drove the pastor home in his own car. By the time we'd gotten to his home he'd confessed everything that'd happened between he and his wife, invited David and I inside for breakfast (we met his wife) and, before we left, they both agreed to meet with our pastor that evening. While I won't go into all the gory details, he took a leave of absence from his church and six months later he and his wife celebrated their thirtieth anniversary together. Praise God!"

The story isn't over just yet!

When it was found that the ladies were leaving their dancing jobs several people in the church stepped up and began canvassing the members of the congregation and other congregations to find them jobs. At least two new programs (one on literacy and one that aided the ladies in getting a GED) were founded because of the outflow of dancers from the strip clubs into churches in the area.

Plus, as guys and gals who were addicted to alcohol or who had turned to the same because they were lonely, depressed, stressed (you name the issue), came to church, Christians stepped up and started several support groups (some of which were simply pipelines to other Christian organizations that had been ministering to others for years – *Christians In Recovery*, *Celebrate Recovery*).

All-in-all, it was a great awakening of the Christian heart and the fruit that was borne from all the evangelism was seen throughout the community.

The moral of these stories is that sometimes, more often than you might think, <u>God uses people just like you</u> to push the envelope of what

Christians think are appropriate ways to minister. So, before you discard a radical idea you might want to ask yourself – is it a radically bad idea or a radically God idea?

Chapter 28

Your Church May Not Be the Right Church For Some

[Note: As I begin this section, I want you, my reader, to know that when I use the terms 'your church' or 'church' in the following paragraphs I'm speaking in the natural rather than in the spiritual. In other words, every Christian knows (or should know) that we (Christians) are the Church (the body of Christ). However, for the sake of ease, I'll use the term church in its most commonly understood form (i.e., a church building).]

You've got to be okay with the fact that not everyone (perhaps not even the majority) of those you meet and witness to about the love of Jesus are going to be comfortable in your church.

For this reason, you should make every effort to connect with multiple churches in your area (attend a few services, get to know the pastors, the elders, the members) so that when you find someone who isn't comfortable with the way your congregation does things you'll know which church to point them to.

Those you minister to need to know that while they're welcome at your church (if they are), attending church isn't mandatory for them to be loved by you. The reason I've placed 'if they are' in parentheses is because, for any number of reasons, the people you meet may not actually be welcome at the church you attend.

For instance, the church my family attends is non-denominational. As such, we're pretty 'free-wheeling' when it comes to the music we listen to and we're really laid back as far as any dress code goes. When I was a Senior Pastor our posted dress code was: *Just Don't Come to Church Naked!* I've attended churches where 20% - 30% of the attendees on Sunday morning were surfers who walked straight in off the beach. This particular church went so far as to have surfboard racks installed on their walls so those who wanted to come would feel 'welcome and at home.' Would the church you attend be okay with that type of fellowship? Maybe. Maybe not. Before you invite someone to attend your church you need to know the answer to this question.

A Bitter Slice of Reality

Sometimes, getting outside the four walls of your church means breaking through barriers you might not even know exist. One of these barriers is a fashion-oriented congregation. Some congregations simply don't want homeless or even shabbily dressed people to come into their buildings. They're fine with helping people as far as serving them by giving donations, feeding, helping them find jobs or getting them healthcare but they don't want people who can't dress *up* to their standards to come to their church. Another congregational barrier I've encountered is ethnically based. In other words, some churches are composed of a majority of one skin color or another and that's the way their members like it.

Cliques inside a church is still another barrier. Such cliques can include but aren't limited to a vast majority of attendees who are very wealthy or poor; who are in the same or similar professions (I know of at least two churches in which the majority of members are physicians or scientists) or who have very well established membership (i.e., members who have gone to the same church since it was founded or even generational members). A very familiar clique to most of us is called a conjugal clique – a church whose membership is primarily made-up of husbands and wives and very few single people (with the exception of their children).

A major problem I've seen with the aforementioned barriers and cliques is that those who don't 'fit in' often feel marginalized, excluded and, sometimes, even judged. While I could rail against churches that allow such behavior to exist (similar to what the Apostle James warned against in James 2:1-5), I doubt that it would do much good. Suffice it to say that if you currently attend such a church you should know that it isn't following the mandate set by God to include everyone and anyone who is His child.

Still, even with all the barriers mentioned above (and many more that weren't), it is possible to either remove these barriers (with a lot of prayer, persistence and God's help) or, at the very least, to expand the same so that the church in question is willing to accept people who are different than they are (socially, educationally, financially, ethnically). Of course, the only way any church is going to break through its walls and spill out into the world is by the wonder working power of God.

Such barriers and cliques can be devastatingly difficult to emotionally deal with if you're a person who is committed to reaching out to your community because you'll probably be doing so without much help from your church. It happens all the time. If you find that this is a barrier you're up against I hope the following story encourages you. What you're about to read is one of the neatest and spiritually caring ministries I've ever witnessed.

Making Certain You've Got a Captive Audience

Bob, an elderly gentleman from a semi-local Baptist church, began a bus ministry for those who can't otherwise make it to church. But, it's a ministry with a twist. Every Saturday and Sunday Bob goes out to various locations in his community, picks up those who want to go to church, drives them to the place of worship they choose to attend and then picks them up and drives them back home.

The 'twist' is that though Bob goes to a very traditional Baptist church he doesn't demand his passengers attend his church. Instead, he'll take them to any church in his area – all while smiling, talking and having a great time with his passengers (many of whom are slightly drunk when he picks them up). His only rule is that everyone who rides in his bus must be polite to everyone else.

During the past three years he's even went so far as to pick up a half dozen or so Jehovah's Witnesses and has taken them to the Kingdom Hall they attended. In doing so he did two things:

● He broke through the image of Christians that the Watchtower Bible and Tract Society promotes (i.e., that Christians are automatically going to 'hate Jehovah's Witnesses because they hate the *real* Jesus').

● Each time Bob drove them to and from a Kingdom Hall he' drive a bit slower than normal and took the time to ask them about what they were going to learn and what they had learned after he picked them up. A discussion always ensued and, as a result, after many, many trips to and from Kingdom Hall's all but one man has converted to Jesus Christ and had started going to a Christian church.

Bob's willingness to do what most people wouldn't has served to break down barriers most other Christians can never get over. I'm certain it also causes Satan to have an absolute fit every time someone accepts Jesus as their Savior.

Chapter 29

God Has a Plan (For Your Life), Satan Has a Plot (Against Your Life)

God wants you to prosper – *radically* – Satan wants you to fail – *miserably*!

Prosperity or similar expressions of the word (tsalach, euodoo, shalom, sakal, etc.) are used over 80 times in the Bible and the definition of the same can be: 'to advance, to make progress, to succeed, to be profitable, to bring to successful issue, to be peaceful (shalom), and to be financially successful.

The majority of the times the words prosper, prosperity, prosperously, prospered etc. are used financial issues aren't being addressed. Rather it is our relationship with God that is the focus.

Read through the Bible and you'll find that God's overall plan for you is one of prosperity and peace that comes from being a part of His kingdom as well as being a joint heir with Jesus! By contrast, Satan's plot is for us to be miserable, in all aspects. Period.

[I'd quickly note the following: The prosperity and peace one has in Jesus will not necessarily translate into immediate, earthly happiness. Sometimes it will but, at other times, as with the Apostle Paul, we'll find ourselves horribly oppressed, hungry, homeless, abused, ill or abandoned. When you find yourself in such situations and you can still rejoice that Christ is your Lord and you are confident God is in control – this is true prosperity and peace.]

When you take a moment to compare even a few of the titles attributed to God versus Satan it's easy to understand the differences.

God	Satan
• God Almighty	• The god of this world
• Creator	• Destroyer
• Friend	• Accuser of our brethren
• Helper	• Adversary
• Good	• Wicked
• Purifier	• Slanderer
• Good Shepherd	• Enemy
• Lover	• Hater
• Shield	• Foe
• Comforter	• Hostile
• The Truth	• Father of lies
• Giver of Life	• Murderer
• Prince of Peace	• Evil one

I bring this up so you'll not be discouraged when things don't seem to be going your way as you attempt to accomplish the will of God. The reason I want you to staunchly refuse to give into doubt, fear or uncertainty is because these emotions are *just emotions*.

I'm not implying Christians should be emotionless. Heaven forbid! God Himself is the most emotion-filled Person in existence and we're made in His image. Instead, we must make certain the emotions we feel are from God and not someone or something else. Without this recognition, emotions (even those with no anchor in reality) can cripple the drive you have, make muddy the clarity of vision God has given you and stall your efforts to do whatever it is God is leading you to do. Again, as you set out to do God's will, it's great to know that everything is in the control of our Lord and Savior – that nothing and no one (not even Satan) can thwart His plans!

Regardless of your skin color, the skill sets you have or where you live you can be instrumental in showing people the love of Jesus in practical ways.

Cast aside any fear or doubt you may have that God can't use you. He can. If you're willing to let Him. I promise.

I'd like to share the BEST piece of advice I've ever gotten from anyone concerning what to do when you don't know what God wants you to do. It was from Jack Little who was, at the time, my pastor.

In brief, I complained, "*Jack, I know God wants me to do something more than I'm doing now but I just don't know what it is I'm supposed to do.*"

Jack looked at me and gave me a piece of advice that has served me very well for the past 15 years. He said:

"*I'm not certain what God wants you to do either. So, until you do know what He wants you to do, why not go out and do those things you know would please Him and that He wouldn't be upset about?*"

It was like a light came on! It made perfect sense to me. I knew, from studying the Bible, those things that He wanted us to do and I had the witness of the Holy Spirit to guide me in not doing those things that might cause Him embarrassment.

I'm convinced Jack's advice was inspired by the Holy Spirit because whenever I've found myself wondering what it is God wants me to do and I've followed it, what I'm supposed to do as a Christian becomes crystal clear.

I believe God can use the times when we're confused as a time of maturing. While we are out and about doing things we might consider menial in nature they are, in reality, building strength of character and core skills.

Serve Inside Before Serving Outside

I'd be remiss in my duties as a minister of the Gospel of Jesus Christ if I didn't share an overarching concern I have with Servant Evangelism.

My concern is that we, as Christians, will become so concerned about those who are in the world (pre-Christians) that we'll lose sight of the fact that there are many who are our own family members (Christians) who need as much and sometimes more help than those who are not yet in the family of Christ.

We'd do well to remember John 13:34-35: *"A new command I give you: <u>Love one another</u>. As I have loved you, so you must love one another. <u>By this all men will know that you are my disciples, if you love one another</u>."*

When pre-Christians see Christians taking care of our own family members, they will want to become part of His family.

With that being said, some of the outreaches I've outlined herein (ministering to strippers, drunks and driving cultists to and from their places of worship) might be out of your comfort zone. Then again, they might be routine for your personality type. Either way, it's okay. Just remember that the old adage, *'You've got to catch them before you can clean them,'* goes for people as much as it does fish.

God doesn't expect anyone to come to Him who is already clean. He expects us to be found as dirty, filthy rags. It is the Father who provides everyone who'll accept them clean garments, washed by the blood of His Son and it is the Holy Spirit who is sent so that He can keep us clean. Our salvation comes from Him and Him alone.

Finally, remember that you, as His child, are told: *"Go therefore and make disciples of all the nations, baptizing them in the name of the Father and the Son and the Holy Spirit, teaching them to observe all that I commanded you."* Matthew 28:19-20a.

So, go forth and LIVE JESUS OUT LOUD! Let everyone in your family, your neighborhood, your city and your church know that you are sold out to the commission Jesus gave us before He ascended to Heaven.

Let Me Know How You're
Living Jesus Out Loud!

Please, take a moment and drop me an email or write me a letter and let me know how you are living Jesus out loud in your community. I can't promise I'll be able to answer you but I will try.

Email: LivingJesusOutLoud@99for1ministries.com

Postal:
99 for 1 Ministries
P.O. Box 180932
Mobile, AL. 36618

I can't wait to hear from you – Rev. Lonnie Honeycutt (RevLon)

ABOUT THE AUTHOR

During the past twenty-five years Lonnie has served as the outreach minister for four churches. He has energetically sought to bring Jesus to those who are 'invisible' (the homeless, prostitutes, drug-users, those in nursing homes) and to those who have become disenfranchised by society.

Ordained as a minister in 2006, Lonnie served briefly as the senior pastor of Deeper Life Fellowship East during which time he was diagnosed with Stage IV cancer of the head and neck and died on February 16, 2008 due to complications associated with his recovery. After being resurrected, he wrote the well-received book *Death, Heaven and Back*. In 2010, he and his wife (Dawn) founded 99 for 1 Ministries – a non-profit organization dedicated to serving those who are under-loved.

Currently Pastor Lonnie is working on his third book, *Living Jesus Out Loud for Families*. He may be contacted for speaking engagements by visiting

www.99for1Ministries.com

or emailing him at:

LivingJesusOutLoud@99for1Ministries.com.

www.ingramcontent.com/pod-product-compliance
Lightning Source LLC
Chambersburg PA
CBHW072340090426
42741CB00012B/2855

9 7 8 0 9 8 8 2 2 0 9 0 4